BIG CHANGE

A 10-STEP PLAN TO LEAD LARGE ORGANIZATIONAL
TRANSFORMATIONS FROM THE INSIDE

STEVE PINKUS

BARLOW

Library and Archives Canada Cataloguing in Publication data available.

ISBN 978-1-988025-00-1 (print)
ISBN 978-1-988025-01-8 (ebook)

Printed in Canada

Cover design: Luke Despatie
Interior design and typesetting: Brady Type

For more information, visit www.barlowbooks.com

Barlow Book Publishing Inc.
96 Elm Avenue, Toronto, ON, Canada M4W 1P2

BARLOW

CONTENTS

The Problem

CHANGE MANAGEMENT is all the rage these days. There are many books and articles written on the subject and many brilliant practitioners and gurus explaining how every change must consider the 'people' element of change. Many organizations have been adding staff and hiring a myriad of consultants to help them address change in all the work they do.

This book isn't about managing all organizational changes. It's about managing the really big changes—the ones I call major organizational *transformations*. 'Transformation projects' significantly change business processes, people processes, and/or major technological capabilities. Typically, they will make or break organizations. Sometimes they are created to help the organization survive. Other times they are created to grow the business or change its strategic direction. Ultimately, they are about organizational survival, whether now or in the future. Some examples are:

- a merger or acquisition

- major organizational restructuring because of required strategic changes

- major organizational restructuring as a result of downsizing or expansion

- a major enterprise technology change required to better operate or compete (e.g., Enterprise Resource Planning [ERP] implementation).

This book is about those make-or-break transformations that organizations have to get right, and about how to do them right. In my experience, there is a serious problem with how these organizational transformations are handled today.

Before we turn to the subject of the book—how transformations can be managed and implemented more effectively and economically—consider these two examples, from my own experience, of what can go wrong.

◉ ◉ ◉

EXAMPLE 1: NO BUY-IN FROM PRESIDENTS

In 2002 I was working for CapGemini Ernst & Young (now Capgemini) as a member of their Change Management practice. We were in early discussions with a major Canadian manufacturing organization on their second attempt at implementing a large SAP project (an ERP technology to integrate and manage their financial, human resource, and logistics operations information). I was asked to speak with the director of the project to determine what some of the problems were in the original implementation, which had been done by a different consulting firm.

The director told me that their CIO had presented the business case to the executive board and received the authority to install and implement the technology across the business, with the goal of having ten thousand users up and running on the new technology in two years.

He continued: "We spent $50 million getting this technology up and running with a large consulting team in place."

But there was a problem. At the end of two years, they had only a miserly two hundred users. How could that be?

The director replied: "What we didn't think about is that the people who really hold the authority in the company are the individual company presidents. No one asked them if they liked the SAP solution and how it was going to affect their business before agreeing to go ahead. As it turned out, none of them liked it. So they simply told us and all their people: don't use it. They found ways to delay and go around the installation, and we simply had to put a hold on things. We didn't take the time to sell the solution to them—and it killed us. What do we do now?"

EXAMPLE 2: CULTURE CLASH

In the early 2000s a large investment bank (Bank A) acquired another investment bank (Bank B) for an undisclosed sum, thought to be between $475 and $600 million. I was on the consulting team and conducted an analysis of potential work-culture transition issues. The project team, which I met with early every morning, was led by one of the executive members of Bank A.

One day I was asked to report my findings and stood up to face the bank executive. I told him that after conducting interviews at several management and staff levels and reviewing the human resource (HR) policies of both organizations, I had discovered that there were some major differences in culture.

Although the policies at Bank A were industry-competitive, they were strict and inflexible in certain HR policy areas, such as working at home and carry-over vacations. In contrast, the policies at Bank B were more lax and the work culture was perceived as more open and accommodating.

The Bank A executive thanked me for the report but made it clear that the culture clash didn't matter to him and that nothing was going to change. To no avail, I warned him that if he didn't address the problem, there was a risk of flight of his prime assets, the investment team at Bank B. "They may not leave today, but watch out a year from now," I told him. The executive stared intently at me—he was not used to being contradicted—and simply said, "Steve, sit down and be quiet." I did exactly that, and my consulting team promptly assigned me to a different role on the team where the executive wouldn't have to look at me at morning meetings.

While the merger seemed to go extremely well for the next few months, a year later I heard from a senior VP at Bank B that some of their best people had moved out in the wake of the merger.

Culture had indeed mattered.

What do these examples have in common?

In each case, the executive leadership hired a well-known, large consulting firm to lead their change and do most of the work implementing it. In each instance, the results were not good—and in one case, disastrous.

Hence, the thesis of this book, which is based on my experience: large consulting firms are great at developing solutions to these problems, but they are really poor at implementing them.

That shouldn't be a surprise. They don't know your business, and they will make the wrong decision time and again. No matter what they say, they do not have 'skin in the game' and won't make decisions with the same care and sensitivity as you will.

To be blunt, there is a financial dimension to all this. Large professional firms are motivated to keep their consultants fully billable as long as possible. It's just human nature and also reflects their business model.

But it means organizations undergoing change can burn through hundreds of thousands, or even millions, of dollars a month when they engage a large consulting team. When the consultants are finished their work, the company not only gets hit with an enormous bill—often double or even triple the original estimate—but also does not get the results it wanted.

And the worst part of it, as I have seen, is that when the organization undergoes another significant change a few years later, it does the same thing again (perhaps with a different, slicker consulting firm)—the very definition of insanity—and the results are the same.

I have been managing big and small change projects for organizations for over twenty years and have learned that there is a right way and a wrong way to proceed. I have written this book to lay out in detail for CEOs and other executive leaders of organizations how to manage these large transformations the right way.

The Short, Secret Solution

Start by hiring an external consulting firm to help develop your change solutions. They are very good at doing this, and they can give you invaluable advice that is worth their fee.

But—and this is the key—*don't hire an external consulting firm to lead the implementation of that change.* Instead, train your operational leaders (your 'A Team') how to lead large change projects. Take them out of their current operational roles and backfill their everyday jobs. Put these operational leaders in charge of your change. You will find that your results will be much better—both in quality and staying on schedule—and you will save millions of dollars, primarily in consulting fees, even with the cost of backfilling the jobs of these operational leaders.

Change is happening at a faster and faster pace. Twenty or thirty years ago, organizations could get away with managing one major change every four or five years, and technology wasn't changing that fast. Managing large change projects now needs to be a core skill of all of your operational leaders.

If you are an executive or accountable for your next major organizational change, you need to read this book. You can't afford to get big change wrong. It could cost you market share price, unacceptable expense losses, turnover of key talent, or even threaten the existence of your organization.

10 Steps to a Successful Organizational Transformation

I have created a 10-Step guide on how to manage large changes in your organization. Not everything is new. A lot of it is simplified, but successful change can still be difficult to accomplish. You may only need to apply some of the steps, or parts of them. All of them can be learned by any operational leader who is leading the change.

The first two steps are about gaining commitment and alignment for the change. They include crucial alerts, points where you need to stop until that step is complete and everyone is on board. This takes courage on the part of the leader and the organization. You won't find this as a formal part of other change management or project management methods.

The remaining eight steps lay out the critical elements of change management and project management activities that leaders—your leaders—need to understand to prepare for, launch, and support major change. I have successfully applied all of the steps in my practice over many years and guarantee you: they all work!

Who Needs to Read This Book

I wrote this book, first, for the executive team of any organization, the ones responsible for making decisions on major changes that must occur in their organization to keep it afloat, to increase market share, or to adjust for major market shifts. Executives shouldn't just read this book when a big change is about to happen. Ideally, they should read it before those changes occur—so they can prepare their operational leaders to lead these changes. All executives need to read this book so they don't make the mistake of abdicating their leadership of a critical transformation to an external team.

The operational leaders of the organization—the directors or senior managers of functions that will be leading the change—will also benefit from reading this book. They will need to be ready for the time when they are called upon to lead the charge in implementing the change.

Once your A Team is committed and getting ready to lead this change, and the next change is announced, executives should encourage the rest of the management team to read this book. You have the best chance for success when all your organizational leaders know the direction in which you are planning to go.

Why Should You Listen to Me?

I have been managing large and small company transformations for over twenty years. I have been part of those large consulting teams, and I have also been on 'cleanup' duty, asked to go in to fix problems others have left behind. I work in the trenches, with all functions, at all levels of the organization to help implement change. I have many certifications. Besides my MBA and PMP, I am also Prosci certified and have advanced Training and Development certification from the OSTD/ASTD, technology certifications in ITIL and Agile, and several others in change management, project management, and other related areas.

I also know the theory. But the truth is: there is a right way to lead large organizational changes, and it doesn't come from theory. Change management and project management approaches have been packaged and repackaged over the years, but I have seen and applied the approach that works—and it works virtually every time. It takes courage and work, but it's the only way if you want quicker, cheaper, and more effective results, as the testimonials from clients on the back cover attest.

My 10-Step Guide

Your organization will achieve successful transformation by following these steps:

STEP 1:   Gain Executive Agreement for the Organizational Transformation

STEP 2:   Assign the Right Team and Develop the Project Plan

STEP 3:   Design and Manage Effective Training and Communication Activities

STEP 4:   Launch the Transformation Project

STEP 5:   Build a High-Performing Transformation Project Team

STEP 6:   Assess the Degree of Support and Resistance for the Transformation Project

STEP 7:   Create a Multi-Pronged Approach in Preparing for Transformation

STEP 8:   Manage the Transformation—Reset the Project Plan at Milestones or Gates

STEP 9:   Prepare for and Support the Transformation Launch

STEP 10: Sustain the Transformation—Create the New Norm

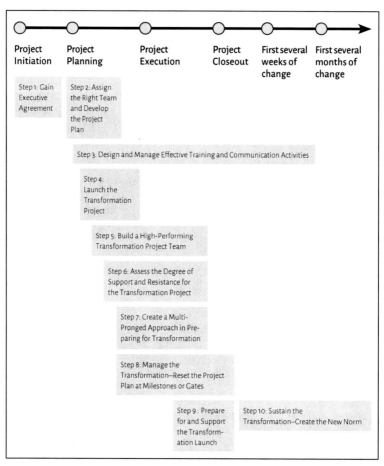

FIGURE 1. *Big Change* 10 Steps mapped to Project Plan phases

Format of the Steps

Steps may need to be implemented sequentially or concurrently. Each step includes:

- a cautionary tale from my own experience
- a description of all the work that needs to be done to complete the step

- tips to help avoid pitfalls and complete the work more effectively and efficiently

- an initial assessment to determine what work needs to be done within the step as it relates to your particular transformation

The 10 Steps should all be understood, but the extent to which the steps/work needs to be done will be a function of how significant and what kind of a transformation is planned.

STOP POINTS

At the end of or within some sections in the 10-Step guide, STOP POINTS are indicated. These are major transformation milestones that, if not achieved, should cause the organization to stop and consider whether it can effectively proceed. From a traditional project point of view, the project would be considered RED and unable to continue until the issue has been resolved or the project is cancelled or put on hold. At each of these points, if the project continues before the specific STOP issue is resolved, the risk of continuing would be either significant overspending, lack of support, and lack of adoption or the implementation of a solution that does not achieve its operational objectives.

NON-TRANSFORMATION WORK

Big Change is focused on preparing for, managing, and sustaining a major organizational transformation. There is other work that will need to be done between steps and within each step that is essential for the solution to work and often specific to the kind of transformation solution being implemented, but that is not covered in this book. For instance, an IT transformation project will require successfully managing and delivering technical solutions; while this work is essential, we will not be addressing it here. When relevant, a NON-TRANSFORMATION WORK note will indicate where and what that work is, but the details of the work will not be covered within the content of this guide.

CHAPTER 1

Step 1: Gain Executive Agreement for the Organizational Transformation

> *If you find a good solution and become attached to it, the solution may become your next problem.*
>
> —Robert Anthony

Your Executive Team has just decided to spend $60 million on new computer technology. See if you relate to this scene: *The CIO has just finished a presentation explaining how this ERP system will improve the productivity of the organization, connect all areas of the business, allow for faster and better decisions, and how you must catch up with the competition in your current systems.* And to what one of the executives is thinking: *He makes it seem like a no-brainer. But only one or two people in the room really understand what this new system will do. No one can really explain the details of the business case or how and when the return of investment will occur. Why is no one asking this?! Sure, the presentation and information is slick and convincing, but ultimately I'll go with the flow and just trust the CIO. I'll agree because I don't really understand this technology stuff. Why do techies always like to show those charts with five hundred connected shapes that you can't even read—are they daring one of us to admit we don't understand it? Safer to say nothing and nod my head. Either this will work and we'll all look good or it'll be the CIO's head on the chopping block, not mine.*

This chapter is about asking the tough questions before you even start, about making sure the Executive Team—every single member—truly understands and believes:

- why there is a problem big enough to risk millions of dollars of investment and disrupt the organization's operations

- that the solution presented is the right one to address this big problem, and really understands it

- in what it will take to implement the solution and how it will impact the organization, their area, and themselves personally

- in what success will look like—what is the prize?—and when it should be expected

Without full commitment and 'skin in the game' from the entire Executive Team, there is a danger that the wrong solution will be chosen. There is also a danger that key senior leaders not being on board will jeopardize the implementation of that solution—the Project Team will need committed resources and support throughout a potentially lengthy and difficult transition period while the solution is implemented.

My Step 1 Story:
Build It and They Will Come

I was the Change Management Lead for a major strategic technology transformation at a Canadian bank. We were implementing a single system to replace several internal systems that had long represented a productivity, quality, and cost burden to this large organization. At first, everything seemed promising. The transformation was led by a senior IT executive, who assigned a senior and experienced Project Manager, and a talented technical team was assembled to develop the detailed solution. A Steering Committee was put in place, representing a good cross-section of senior executives from across the organization. The goal of the project was to design and implement a full solution for all current users of the legacy systems being replaced, across all business units. This transformation would affect 7,000 people across the organization. My first task was to determine who the stakeholder base really was and interview senior stakeholders to find out what their support level, issues, and concerns were. After doing this work, I discovered the following:

- Although a full solution was being developed for all current users, about 90% to 95% of users were IT users. The current business culture and processes created a unique situation where the IT department not only supported the legacy system but also were the key users entering data and producing reports for their respective business units. Therefore, the legacy system was designed by the IT department for IT users.

- The goal of the new system replacing the existing legacy system was to manage every aspect of their project work. It was designed for business users and had a lot of built-in self-service elements. The longer-term vision was to expand the user base to business users across the business—another seven thousand non-technical people—most of whom were not current users. This second group of users was not included in the project. The approach of the IT executive entrusted to drive this transformation was "build it and they will come." She believed that if they built a system that was being successfully used by thousands of IT users, it would be enthusiastically accepted. Why consult them?

- This course of action had happened before. As a result, the non-IT parts of the business often developed their own systems and processes to meet their specific needs. There was skepticism about the planned transformation and concern that the past would repeat itself. Also, the current legacy processes related to the systems being replaced were considered cumbersome and inappropriate for the nimble business processes that were needed in their business areas.

I presented this information to the Project Manager and Project Sponsor and tried to make a case for them to reconsider their transformation strategy. (NOTE: The Project Manager was responsible for managing all Project Team resources, and the Project Sponsor was the executive accountable for the overall success of the project. More on these roles in Step 2.) I told them the data I collected suggested there was not true buy-in among executives beyond the IT executive functions and that the Steering Committee did not truly represent a full cross-section of the stakeholder group in the final transformation solution vision. They—particularly the Sponsor—did not like my story.

The Project Sponsor (I will call her Diane) was a mid-level, extremely overworked bank VP who was delegated the role of Sponsor by her Executive VP and told to just get it done. Diane's area was severely under-resourced, having lost several key managers and not received approvals to replace them. I realized quickly that it should have really been her boss (I will call her Elaine) leading this effort and her boss's head on the line for this project, not hers. Diane and the Project Manager believed that the strategy was set and supported by the Steering Committee, which, they believed, represented the full business. I had personally interviewed all Steering Committee members—half were IT representatives from the other business areas and half of the remaining members had the same concerns as mentioned above.

The Project Manager and Project Sponsor were not happy that I had raised a red flag and that there was serious project risk because senior support had not been properly attained. The project had already been running for many months before I arrived, much of the budget had been spent, and there was increased commitment within the IT project sponsorship group and management. Diane stated: "The solution is set. Elaine has made it clear that our job is to implement, not question, the solution. Your job is to help make it work."

To compound matters, Diane was an invisible leader to most in her department. She had an office on the same floor as most of her staff, but the office was tucked around a wall near the doors by the elevators. Getting on her calendar for a discussion was a challenge too. My supposedly regular meetings set up to discuss urgent project matters were often bumped.

This lack of support caused many delays and changes of scope to the Project Plan as it moved forward. The jury is still out on whether the business will eventually buy into the final transformation solution, as it is a multi-year implementation, but early signs are not good.

Step 1 Activities

All executive teams must accomplish the critical actions in this step before they move forward with a major transformation project.

Step 1 is about creating both clarity in the solution and consensus for urgency in spending the required time and resources to effectively launch the transformation project. Every executive who will be affected or who controls budget and resources required to prepare, implement, and sustain the transformation must agree to and understand the time, resources, and budget related to the transformation project. The Executive Team includes the 'crossover manager.' This is the one executive who manages all other executives affected by the proposed transformation. This is often the CEO but may be a COO or other executive in a very large organizational structure. The crossover manager is often left out of Step 1.

Frequently, a transformation project begins with an initial top-executive discussion on the need for the transformation, followed by the assignment of a mid-level lead to run with the project and occasionally report back to the top-level Executive Team on progress. Since this project is being identified as a strategic need, this approach is not a delegation of project activities; it is an abdication of executive responsibility. The executive crossover manager and top-level team must understand and buy into the solution as much as other affected executives/senior managers. They should be involved in every stage of Step 1 described below. Think about this. Why on earth should a major transformation project—one that will make or break the organization's viability or strategic growth—be led from anywhere but the executive office?

Be Clear on WHY the Change Is Needed

In other words: Why spend the money, expend the effort, and take the risk of changing?

Transformational change is difficult. It takes money, resources, and long-term commitment, and there is always a risk of failure. All senior executives must agree that the rewards are worth the risk and commit that they will meaningfully contribute to the organization's top-level strategy.

Up front, the Executive Team must create clear and compelling statements that fill in the following blanks:

1. "If we don't change 'X' by 'Y' time, then an unacceptable 'Z' will happen."

2. "If we change 'X,' then we will achieve competitive advantage 'A.'" (i.e., we will be vaulted ahead in the market)

3. "If we don't change 'X,' then we won't meet strategic business objective 'A.'"

Both of the first two points must be viewed as an essential organizational activity from the point of view of ALL senior executives. For the project to proceed, the third point must be true and resonate with every executive affected by the change.

These statements must be stated in quantitative terms and with clear timelines.

ALL senior executives affected by, or who could affect, the change/transformation must agree on the necessity for change.

STOP POINT

The project is dead in the water if consensus is not achieved at this initial point. If the transformation is essential for organizational survival, then it must be discussed until agreement is achieved. If the CEO believes that the solution is essential for organizational survival and there is persistent resistance in certain quarters, then perhaps a tough decision should be made on changing executive team members. If it is a critical transformation but not essential for survival, then the project might be able to be deferred until other more urgent company objectives are achieved. If the business issue or reason to launch the transformation project does not relate to a 'top 5' strategic business priority, then it does not qualify as a major transformation. This first part of Step 1 must be completed before expending the energy in developing a transformation solution.

NON-TRANSFORMATION WORK
CREATE THE RIGHT TRANSFORMATION SOLUTION
Once there is executive agreement, then an individual or small team should be assigned to design an effective solution. It is assumed that

the organization will arrive at a good solution, but if it doesn't, it will be seriously scrutinized in the next step! Here are some tips to help guide the individual or small group assigned to developing the right transformation solution.

1. Interview all executives who will be most affected or impacted as 'internal customers,' and conduct a thorough requirements review. Develop a comprehensive view of what should be addressed from all business perspectives in creating an effective business solution.

2. Assign a tight turnaround time to present the solution to executives. If there is a true strategic need, it should be urgent. Also, strategic priorities change, and what is an organizational imperative today may not be tomorrow. Tomorrow the need might not only be different but might also be an even more serious business issue created by the lack of action today.

3. Involve the right individual or team. Ideally, the best individual to lead, or at least be a part of choosing the solution, is the same individual who will lead the transformation project once it is formally launched. Keep the team as small as possible and the efforts under wraps until a solution is developed and agreed to by all executive stakeholders. This individual should be one of your leaders and the team should be comprised of your own staff people, not a consultant and his or her people. Use consultants as expert advisors, not as front-line leaders spearheading activities.

Clarify What Will Change

Once the solution has been developed and selected, it must be communicated and sold to the Executive Team. It is important to provide clear and honest expectations about how the organization, business functions, and individuals will be affected by the change. Even though much will be unknown at this early stage, the following information is essential.

WHAT TECHNOLOGY WILL CHANGE?

- If the transformation project is a technology project or is technology driven, ensure there is full understanding of how the new system differs from the legacy system(s) that the project will replace.

- Explain what other systems will be affected, interfaces will need to be built, hardware and services will need to be installed, and different support will be required.

- Be honest in the challenges, risks, and unknowns that you will face (e.g., problems with existing data, unknown or 'unchartered waters' in developing interface solutions).

- Describe the solution in simple language. Don't use acronyms, IT concepts, or complicated architecture pictures. Relate the solution to business needs and strategic priority. IT transformation projects are *business* transformation projects. Make sure IT leaders are talking about the solution in business terms.

WHAT BUSINESS PROCESSES WILL CHANGE?

- Develop current and future state process flows in each part of the business that will need to change to make the transformation successful.

- Highlight process steps that will be modified, added, or deleted.

HOW WILL PEOPLE BE AFFECTED BY THE CHANGE?

- Who will need to be trained on what new technology? (Is there any prerequisite knowledge going from legacy to new systems/technology?)

- Who will need to be trained on new processes?

- How will roles be affected?

  ◊ Will there be any job elimination?

  ◊ Will there be any job modification? Will job modification cause different skill- and salary-level jobs?

  ◊ Are there union or HR considerations for any of these changes?

  ◊ Will business culture change?

- State expected risks and potential issues that will need to be monitored and overcome. The worst scenario for your transformation project is to present a significant unwanted surprise to the senior Executive Team late in the project, especially one that should have been foreseen.

PRESENT A PICTURE OF THE FUTURE STATE

My experience is that senior executives often do not understand the solution, what really will change in the organization, and their function once the change is implemented. Therefore, it is important to describe what the first three to six months after launching the transformation will look like in the following two key areas:

- Training and coaching support: How long will it take the organization to become proficient?

- The productivity 'dip': Typical productivity measures (efficiency and effectiveness) will dip below the before-the-change norm before rising above that norm. This is due to ramp-up time on skills and proficiency and to working out the kinks in new processes and systems. If this expectation is not set early, senior executives may be anxious to pull the plug or may assess the transformation as unsuccessful very soon after launch. Good preparation will dramatically minimize this dip, a point presented to executives in Chapter 2 (Assign the Right Team and Develop the Project Plan).

Conduct a Resource Capacity Assessment

A senior project manager wanted to hire me to help with a major technology implementation at a medium-sized manufacturing company. After a brief conversation, it became clear to me that there were many other projects going on in his organization, a good number needing the same resources as this project. I told him that I could not in good conscience take this assignment until a thorough resource capacity exercise was conducted to ensure, before starting the project, that resources were available. I also warned him that the project could be delayed or cancelled if this assessment was done and the results uncovered a lack of available resources to be successful. I ended up conducting a resource capacity assessment for this project with the executive group of the organization. The decision? The project would take place but would be delayed one year until critical resources were available. A resource capacity assessment consists of the following activities:

- Determine what the work effort and resources required will be at a macro level.

- Gain commitment for internal resources required. Include both Project Team resources and the time commitment that other functions' resources will need to give throughout the project (e.g., subject-matter experts, Super Users, and other early training resources).

- Gain commitment for external resources required.

- Gain commitment for other project expenses required (e.g., project office, software/hardware).

- Build in time and resources contingencies (Project Plans can only be accurately assessed at between twelve and twenty-four weeks at a time; any longer and they are most often underestimated).

STOP POINT

The Executive Team must thoroughly understand the transformation solution and the impact it will have on the organization, their function, and themselves. The Project Manager needs to test this by having individual discussions with senior executives before and/or after presenting the solution to ensure full understanding and to highlight their concerns and risks. It is highly possible that when the senior team fully understands all elements of the solution chosen, they will be uncomfortable with it. If there is not total executive buy-in for the solution developed, you must either discuss the solution until an agreement is achieved or the solution is reworked. If this is not a painful and difficult exercise, you probably aren't doing it openly and honestly. Moving forward without this commitment is one of the leading causes for project failure.

_____

Select a Project Sponsor

Once there is agreement, a senior executive must be assigned as the 'Project Sponsor' of the change (the transformation should become a key performance objective for that executive in the short and long term).

The accountabilities of an active Project Sponsor must be specifically defined. The executive assigned must understand and know what he or she is signing up for. Key accountabilities are:

- facilitating consensus among all executive stakeholders throughout the life of the project

- communicating the new priorities to the organization

- providing the reinforcement required to ensure success

- ensuring resources requirements are met

Project Sponsors must understand that they are signing up for a very active role, not one that can be delegated to a Project Manager who will report progress to them. It will take dedicated weekly time, require visibility as the 'face' of the project, and should become a key objective in their personal performance measures rather than an undocumented task that has been delegated to them as extra work that is not part of their 'real' job.

_____

STOP POINT

There are different philosophies and methodologies on managing change; however, almost every change methodology and change practitioner firmly believes that one of the biggest causes of failed transformation is the lack of effective sponsorship. There is no way to continually keep the transformation a strategic priority among an executive group without a sponsor who is tenaciously and constantly fighting for it to remain a tier-one project. The project should not be launched or should not continue without the right strong, active sponsor chosen to lead the project. If the right sponsor "doesn't have time," this is proof that the Executive Team isn't convinced. Stop until this is resolved!

Set Up a Project Steering Committee

The Executive Team must formally commit to offering resources and money and to keeping the project a continued strategic priority throughout the life of the project. The best way to accomplish this is to set up a Steering Committee to oversee the project, make major decisions, and resolve escalated risks and issues.

Membership should consist of:

- all senior executives whose function is affected by the transformation project

- a senior executive who acts as a Transformation Project Advocate (a senior executive who is a clear active supporter of the transformation and who is willing to assist the Project Sponsor and the Project Manager/Project Team in actively and visibly promoting and supporting the transformation project)

- the Project Sponsor, who will be the chair of the Steering Committee and will be at least at the same organizational level as the other Steering Committee members

Set up a meeting schedule for the life of the project (throughout the preparation, launch, and for at least three to six months after the transformation project solution is launched). A good rule of thumb is to meet monthly, with the expectation that ad hoc meetings may be needed for major project decisions or major project issues requiring immediate decision-making.

A lot of Steering Committees are ineffective and are run like glorified project team meetings. Executives/Senior Leaders are not interested in progress reporting on project details. The only things that should be presented to this group are information to help clarify key components of the solution, items requiring executive decisions, and high-level milestone achievements/progress—ideally, all in a one-page scorecard.

◼ ◼ ◼

Once real executive buy-in occurs, a Senior Sponsor is assigned, and Project Governance is put in place, you are ready to proceed to Step 2. But make sure you get Step 1 right! Note that Step 1 only involves a small group of executives or senior people and that there is more than one occasion when the project might need to be stopped, cancelled, or modified. I cannot overemphasize how important this step is for the success of your transformation project. My experience is that the number-one reason for projects failing to work and achieve adoption among employees in the workforce is that Step 1 was omitted or implemented poorly.

CHAPTER 2

Step 2: Assign the Right Team and Develop the Project Plan

What counts is not necessarily the size of the dog in the fight—it's the size of the fight in the dog.

—Dwight D. Eisenhower

THE RIGHT PROJECT MANAGER can make things happen. The wrong one will manage schedules, miss key issues and risks, and not properly support the team. Team members should be fully dedicated subject-matter experts who know their role, know how their work fits in the solution, and believe in the ultimate objectives of the project. This chapter is about how to find and develop internal senior Project Managers within the organization and to effectively equip them to lead major transformation projects.

This is the second of three chapters dedicated to effectively setting up the transformation project before the team even begins its work. Chapter 2 identifies what key roles must be established prior to launching the transformation project work and the characteristics of ideal candidates for these roles. This chapter also identifies the primary initial activity of this core Project Team—creating a Macro Project Plan—and describes what content should be in this plan. The Macro Project Plan is used to determine the work, capabilities, and work volume of the project. The chapter ends with the development of a Project Charter as the main guiding document for your transformation, along with the construction of the detailed Project Plan.

My Step 2 Story: Can a Good Project Manager Manage Any Kind of Project?

Many years ago, I sat in on a discussion with a colleague who became one of my mentors on how to do 'good project management.' She was having a debate with another senior Project Manager on what makes a good Project Manager. This other senior Project Manager talked about how he had managed every kind of project and believed that a good Project Manager really could manage any type of project. He believed that what is really required to do good project management is sound knowledge of the project management process and techniques and experience in how to find and manage resources.

My colleague listened patiently but started to slowly shake her head. She told him that she disagreed with that approach. She believed that good Project Managers must have more than good generic project management knowledge and experience. They must also have enough content knowledge of the project, and of the functions they are managing, to truly manage the project. Project Managers must be able to look at their Functional Leads and their plans or activities and know whether what is being presented is reasonable. The two seasoned Project Managers continued to discuss their philosophies and ended by agreeing to disagree. I, however, was convinced that my colleague and mentor's philosophy was correct. I had seen how she and other competent Project Managers effectively kept our project on course by continuously digging into issues and challenging Project Team work and accomplishments.

A Project Manager who has only generic skills and no knowledge of the project solution or the Project Team functional areas is really a Project Coordinator, ensuring work is properly scheduled and completed. The Project Manager must truly manage the project by uncovering and solving issues and challenges and by knowing enough to continually remove obstacles and support his/her team members in getting their work done. I have tried to apply this same philosophy to my consulting practice. Several times clients have asked me to manage technical IT development and IT installation projects, stating that my project management skills should allow me to manage those projects effectively. Each time one of these projects is presented to me, I decline the offer. I do not know enough about IT software development to be an effective Project Manager for such projects.

Step 2 Activities

For the reasons presented in my story above, putting the right Project Team together starts with putting the right Project Manager in place. The Project Manager's first task should be to select Project Leads to represent key areas of major activities. The initial core team should be selected carefully, conservatively erring on the side of under-resourcing until needs are clearly established when creating the Project Plan (discussed later in this chapter). The Project Manager then leads the process of creating a Project Charter and detailed Project Plan, which include data of the type of work and volume of work required to guide the Project Manager in hiring other technical and support individuals.

Assign the Right Project Manager

This is the most important role on the team. The Project Manager for a major transformation must be a passionate, energetic, and talented leader. Although the Project Sponsor will be the formal face of the transition, the Project Manager will be the engine that runs it.

ASSIGNING AN INTERNAL PROJECT MANAGER

It is always preferable to assign an internal Project Manager to lead a major transformation. This is a major tenet of the *Big Change* philosophy:

> Leading transformation projects is a core organizational competency that needs to be developed throughout all organizations.

The only constant organizations should expect is that change never stops. Organizations must know how to manage and implement change successfully if they are to be successful. Farming out the management of a major organizational transformation is like farming out the development of a marketing or business strategy to another firm to manage. Organizations seek external consulting expertise and help for their marketing and business strategies and continue internally to manage and develop these core competencies to manage their business. Yet these same organizations don't treat the management of major transformations the same way.

Your own people know the business and the organization better than any consultant and will make better, more passionate Project Managers. The right Project Manager will be the candidate who has the advantage of understanding the business and knowing the business culture and its people. It is a huge advantage.

Your internal Project Manager is known to your people. This is important because it establishes trust. If the Project Manager is a known entity, especially someone perceived as an effective manager and leader by key senior stakeholders, you have greater potential of gaining support for the program and of being confident it will succeed. The result will be fewer issues and less resistance.

The ideal Project Manager candidate should possess a number of qualities and demonstrated ability. He or she should have a solid knowledge of the business and its operations; be a strong, honest 'driver'; possess courage and stamina; and be a good communicator.

Hiring an External Project Manager

An external Project Manager should only be hired because no one inside the organization has the necessary experience or meets the required criteria. And because the organization needs its own senior leaders to develop that skill. If you hire an external Project Manager, assign your best internal candidate as co-Lead on the transformation project so they can learn while working alongside the external resource.

A qualified external Project Manager has done this kind of project before in a similar industry and under similar circumstances. There is nothing worse than an outside 'expert' coming into an organization whom people perceive as an elite consultant and who really doesn't understand their business or their issues, or one who appears too theoretical and who doesn't 'speak their language.' Establishing credibility and trust is paramount.

The external Project Manager must also know every part of the project being managed, be seen as taking charge and creating urgency, and establish themselves quickly as a leader. The Project Manager must be a good communicator at every level of the organization and with the Project Team.

The Project Manager must also be a good coach because an important part of the job should be to mentor potential Project Managers for future major transformations. Assign your most promising leaders of the future to work alongside this 'ringer' you are bringing in. You should only have to hire externally once and maybe provide coaching in the future.

If you have the perfect internal candidate and they are 'too busy' to be extracted from the business, reassess your commitment to the change as a strategic priority. Either this transformation is important or it is not. If you assign your 'B Team' to manage it, you will get B Team results. If it is truly a strategic priority, it is worth temporarily backfilling this perfect candidate to enable him or her to take on this role. If they are working on another key strategic transformation or strategic priority, then perhaps it is time to develop more internal

Transformation Project Managers/Leaders. Hire the external Project Manager, train the internal development candidate, and assign the candidate as co-Lead. A major strategic transformation project needs your top organizational talent and attention or it will fail.

If you think your organization would need to hire an external Project Manager for a transformation project, start laying the groundwork. Identify a core group of operational leaders now and get them trained on the 10 Steps to take full mentorship advantage of an external Project Manager.

And a final bit of advice: ensure that an external hire believes in and understands this 10-Step methodology and is willing to mentor your leaders throughout the life of the project.

Develop the High-Level Project Plan

The first task for the Project Manager is to develop a High-Level Project Plan for the transformation project. A High-Level Project Plan is not the same as a typical Project Plan. A typical Project Plan is designed to show all work tasks, dependencies, and resources at a detailed level for the purpose of managing all deliverables in the project. It presupposes that all resources are in place and that all work can be defined. The typical Project Plan requires input from all team resources to be accurate.

The High-Level Project Plan is what it sounds like: a higher-level plan developed by the Project Manager with the objective of then assigning the key project resources required to launch the project and create the more detailed, typical Project Plan. These key project resources are called the Core Project Team.

Assign the Core Project Team

The Core Project Team does not represent the total resources required for the transformation project but consists of all Project Team Leads and key technical or functional specialists required to complete the detailed Project Plan and assign the rest of the team. It represents the 'bare bones' skeleton team that the Project Manager needs in place to complete the initial Project Plan.

Taking into consideration all of the factors related to the detailed Project Plan (see "Create the Detailed Project Plan" below), the Project Manager's goal is to put together a strong Core Project Team, which will deliver each section of the High-Level Project Plan. To that end, the Project Manager assigns or hires:

- Project Leads in each major work package/work stream area

- key Technical Leads

- key Functional Leads (those individuals who have, or will develop, expertise on the solution or elements of the solution from a business process point of view)

Key Functional Leads are a big miss in many transformation projects. Many transformation projects fail because these experts are not specifically assigned, and organizations either give Technical Leads double duty or just omit the role. The result is that a critical process review is left out of the Plan and/or is compressed as a lower priority task.

Ensure that internal individuals are assured that their jobs are secured (if being backfilled) and that this assignment is a career-building assignment versus a career risk. Work with the Project Sponsor to make sure these promises are truly organizational commitments. Without these assurances, internal team assignments are often performed with mediocrity, turn team members into flight risks, and/or create team tension and discord.

Once the Macro Project Plan is complete and the Core Project Team is in place, the Project Manager works with the Team to develop the detailed Project Plan.

Create the Detailed Project Plan

After you gain broad executive support for the need of a transformation solution and pull together a good core team and governance structure for getting the work done, it is time for the Core Project Team to develop a detailed Project Plan and Project Charter.

Your detailed Project Plan should include the following:

- a description of all major streams of work, which may include the following major functions: all technical architecture, design, and development work

- data management and integration

- interface development

- process review or re-engineering

- communication

- human resource activities (e.g., organization restructuring, reclassification of roles, union negotiations and notifications)

- testing (e.g., system, integration, user acceptance)

- training (e.g., course development, delivery, administration)

- maximum number of people required (i.e., the human resources required to complete the heaviest workload)

Develop the Project Charter

It is important to develop a comprehensive and compelling Project Charter to create a deeper understanding of the transformation solution for executive stakeholders and to act as the overall guiding document for getting your project work done. Your Project Charter will be your 'go-to' document, which you will refer to time and time again to test whether you are on track and to remind senior stakeholders of the objectives, goals, and scope of your project.

Creating a Project Charter should be "Project Management 101" for any experienced Project Manager. However, I have found the following problems when assessing how other organizations have performed this step:

- There is no Project Charter, or it is incomplete.

- It is too detailed or technical and, therefore, too comprehensive. I have seen technology projects deliver Project Charters of one-hundred-plus pages to senior executives, filled with technical specifications and jargon. No one ever reads them. The results range from the Charter not being read or understood to a significant delay of project launch.

- There is no executive involvement in the review and sign-off. A good Project Charter should include discussions with executives to both check for understanding and solicit input.

A good Project Charter must include these key elements:

- a clear and comprehensive description of the project need and measurable goals and deadlines (don't just describe the project, be clear on objectives)
- a clear and comprehensive description of what is changing (technology, process, and people)
- a comprehensive listing of scope, including:
  - milestones and/or 'gating' points
  - all technology and/or services that are to be delivered
  - all elements of required transformation work listed in this methodology
  - a section on communication
  - a section on training
  - a section on all human resource activities required if roles are to be eliminated, added, and/or modified
  - a section describing key transformation challenges and the work to address it
- a comprehensive listing of risks to be managed
- a clear Project Governance structure
  - Project Organization Chart (Sponsor and Steering Committee at the top; the Steering Committee should include each senior executive affected by the project/ transformation)
  - Governance Process (team meetings and team communication, Steering Committee and oversight meetings, escalation process)
  - Governance Principles
  - assignment of project 'advocates' if available

CHAPTER 3

Step 3: Design and Manage Effective Training and Communication Activities

Excellence is an art won by training and habituation. We do not act rightly because we have virtue or excellence, but we rather have those because we have acted rightly. We are what we repeatedly do. Excellence, then, is not an act but a habit.

—Aristotle

Think like a wise man but communicate in the language of the people.

—William Butler Yeats

T HIS IS THE FINAL of three chapters dedicated to setting up the transformation project before the team begins its work. Training and communication could be considered part of the overall plan (Step 2), part of the multi-pronged approach to preparing for transformation (Step 7), and a key part of managing the whole 10-Step process. However, it is so critical and unique to managing a successful transformation that I've dedicated Step 3 to developing and managing these activities.

My Step 3 Training Story: Train Me Now or Train Me Later

I was the Change Management Lead for a major ERP technology implementation in the health care industry. I had been brought in as a senior advisor well after the project was launched. Change management activities, including training and communication, were already planned and being implemented by separate Project Leads. It was about three or four months before the first launch of a multi-phased ERP implementation.

After about a week on the project, I met with the Training Lead for the Project Team (I'll call her Simone). I noticed two things right away. First, Simone appeared to be extremely competent and experienced in designing and delivering training for large ERP and other types of IT implementations. Second, she seemed frustrated and tense as she described their training strategy and status. I immediately began probing by asking Simone what her key challenges were and whether there were things about her role and deliverables that were of concern to her. Those questions opened the floodgates. Simone shared her current frustrations and concerns about delivering a high-quality training effort by telling me the following:

- Training designers could not get hold of the completed configured solution in time to properly design customized training for users by the pre-launch training deadline.

- Project budget overruns resulted in the Project Manager deciding to cut training designer and training delivery resources. Almost everyone on Simone's Training Team had their contracts shortened to meet budget cuts. (Simone noted that the team got slashed more severely than any other technical team.)

- A decision was made by the project leadership to severely cut customization of the training solution to meet deadlines with fewer resources. For instance, process changes identified in process review sessions would not be included in exercises or be used as examples of how work got done. Instead, a generic training course would be offered that only focused on how the technical functions worked. The Project Manager had been heard to say: "If worse comes to worst, we can offer generic packaged training for modules that we haven't finished. A lack of customized training never stopped a project from going live ... we will just provide a little more coaching and hand-holding when the system goes live."

- A train-the-trainer solution had been agreed to early on in the project. However, to save costs, it had been decided to train all trainers at the same time at the same place. This meant that some trainers supporting sites of later phases would be trained many months before their system went live (and before they had access to the system to practise what they learned).

Simone remained quite concerned that because of these challenges training would not be successful and would not properly prepare users at go-live time. Simone's experience was that when users do not feel adequately trained, they are fearful and unhappy at the time of launch, which could significantly affect user adoption.

I totally agreed with Simone's assessment, and we immediately began to strategize ways of mitigating the biggest risk areas. Simone was successful in solving some of these problems, including building in some customization (with help from the vendor) and modifying the train-the-trainer approach. Unfortunately, the mitigating solutions came at the expense of a lot of around-the-clock working for many weeks by Simone and her small team.

Step 3 Activities: Training

One of the root causes of resistance for major organizational transformations is lack of adequate training.

Training activities typically begin too late and are assigned less budget and fewer resources than required. The following are critical considerations and actions in developing a training plan that will effectively support your transformation.

Technology Transformation Projects

One of the leading causes of lack of adoption in technology transformation projects is late or inadequate training. In many technology projects, technical activities (e.g., technical design, technical interface development, hardware purchase and refinement, and testing) are often the only work that's considered core project work. This perception causes a bias in many Project Managers to limit budget, resources, and project time to the critical item of training. "Build it and they will come" may have worked in *Field of Dreams*, but it doesn't work in a transformation project. Understanding this point, as an effective Transformation Project Manager, you must quickly identify training as one of your core training deliverables. If you don't train people properly, you don't go live. Period.

The other challenge presented to the Project Manager and team is that training requirements are often not identified until all design work is completed and tested. Timeline pressure to launch the project in a reasonable period of time often causes Project Managers to compress training time. The Project Manager, Project Sponsor, and all senior executives must agree that training is a Critical Path activity, understand the work and timing of each major activity, and understand the consequences of not completing these activities successfully. The best-designed system in the world is useless if users of the system don't quickly become proficient in using it. This fact seems so obvious that I am continually amazed that training activities are so often compressed or omitted.

The Project Manager should ensure that the following critical elements of a comprehensive training plan are considered:

Create realistic timelines and budget for designing training Project timelines are often imposed tightly, and training is often at the tail end of the project and at risk of being minimized. Ratios of design time to delivery time vary from 6:1 to 15:1 (six hours of training design time for every hour of training delivery) for determining your design time needs, depending on complexity and training media used. Use internal or external training development experts to estimate all design time needs. To make the Critical Path as short as possible, determine the earliest you can begin design. One effective way to do this is to have training course designers work with solution designers so they can develop materials as close to real time as possible.

Create realistic timelines and budget for delivering training It is tempting to save time and money by scheduling mass web-based training sessions when face-to-face training is required.

Create realistic timelines and budget for post-launch coaching and support No matter how good the training is, people learning new skills are never immediately proficient. They will need support initially until they transition into new ways of working.

Create a long-term plan for continuous skills development on the new system Learning is never complete. Staff need continuous reinforcement and development toward becoming expert.

Train the Project Team first Project Team members should become experts in new processes, technology, and/or skills to effectively support the organization as it prepares for the change.

Identify ALL users who will need to learn new skills very early in the process Conduct a comprehensive assessment early in the project to ensure everyone impacted by the transformation receives appropriate training.

Identify Super Users Within each area of the business where users will require training, identify small groups of employees who will be trained much earlier to be early local experts, or

Super Users. This is often a challenge since customized training materials are often not developed until much too late in the process. One way to address this challenge is to involve these hand-picked future experts in process review work, early design work, and testing and to provide them with whatever generic training is available.

Identify prerequisite training   This needs to be done early, since users will need to be trained on prerequisite training before the core technical training begins. Are users moving from one similar system to another? Or are many of them moving from no system, or spreadsheets, to a new enterprise system that requires a completely new set of skills and knowledge?

Build in process training if business processes are changing   A typical big omission in the training stream of work for transformation projects is omitting the development of process changes within the training course. Training Leads often have their work defined narrowly, only teaching users to use new software and systems. Technical training is often the easier and less important part of the transformation. Training must be aligned with systems design work and process review work. Training Leads must be given the mandate to provide for ALL learning requirements to make the transformation successful.

Use real company examples   Users will not relate to generic, non-industry examples.

Trainers must understand the business   Either train internal trainers early or have external trainers spend time receiving orientation and training on the business.

Conduct face-to-face classroom training where new skills are being learned   It is more difficult and costly to conduct classroom training. For training that doesn't involve teaching very new skills to a savvy and motivated group, web-based self-learning can work well. However, technology transformation projects often involve training user groups in areas where they have never used such a system and they truly need to learn new skills. Self-learning can be frustrating when you need to ask questions, and motivation can be a problem—and ultimately, adoption will suffer.

Create a practice "sandbox" before going live   This is often costly and sometimes impractical, but allowing users to practise before putting in real data pays big dividends in early user adoption. Edward de Bono claims that the 'learning curve' that people know is really inaccurate. That learning curve looks like this:

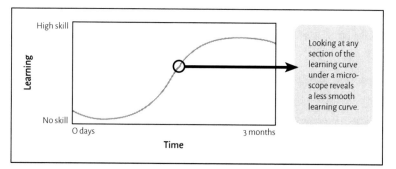

FIGURE 2. The learning curve according to Edward de Bono

It suggests that people learn slowly, and then at some point after practice, learning starts to take hold and accelerate. De Bono says that if you could look at the learning curve through a microscope, it would look like this:

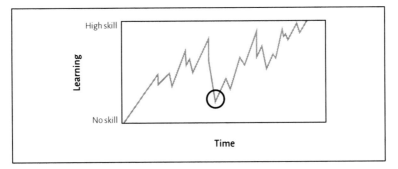

FIGURE 3. A close-up view of one point on the de Bono learning curve

The line on the graph is very jagged, with a lot of little peaks followed by small drops and one very large drop. De Bono says that every one of those peaks occurs after a failure by learners who have just learned a new task. The drop in learning/understanding occurs because learners have lost confidence in their perception of what they know, and subsequent actions prove that their knowledge drops. The really big drop is a monumental mistake ... these are the kinds of mistakes we make where we get a sick feeling in the pit of our stomach that tells us we really screwed up—that we made an error that could have a disastrous outcome. After those types of errors, the learner's "knowledge" (or perception of what they think they know) plummets to a very low level.

The key to quick learning is to allow learners to experience failure without repercussion, so they won't be afraid to try again. Provide a safe training environment for learners so they can practise until they are confident. For new computer technology, these safe environments are often called "sandboxes." Sandboxes, or practice environments, are invaluable for allowing learning to occur more quickly and creating more positive energy about the new system or technology being introduced.

Check that your Training Leads are using the optimum approach Demonstrate ➔ Users try with coaching correction ➔ Users try again with coaching correction ... Repeat until users are confident.

Use non-technical jargon in training The use of technical jargon is a common error in technical training. Test your training with an audience that has no technical background or knowledge before rolling it out to the general population.

Conduct level 1 and level 2 evaluations Evaluate how well training went and how well it was retained.

Develop a user Community of Practice Many organizations have found that they can create both quicker proficiency and adoption by launching what is called a Community of Practice (CoP) within their organization. A CoP is a "group of people who share a concern or a passion for something they do and learn how to do it better as they interact regularly."[1]

DO NOT use generic vendor training Only if the vendor has developed industry-specific examples or there are virtually

---

1   Etienne Wenger, *Communities of Practice, A Brief Introduction*, at https://scholarsbank.uoregon.edu/xmlui/bitstream/handle/1794/11736/A%20brief%20introduction%20to%20CoP.pdf?sequence=1&isAllowed=y.   The group can evolve naturally because of the members' common interest in a particular domain or area, or it can be created specifically with the goal of gaining knowledge related to their field. It is through the process of sharing information and experiences with the group that the members learn from each other and have an opportunity to develop themselves personally and professionally.

no customization or system adaptations available should you consider generic vendor training as an option.

DO NOT rely solely on self-eLearning modules for major technical training for new users Face-to-face learning is more expensive and time-consuming, but it is worth its weight in gold for better and faster learning and proficiency and increased motivation and enthusiasm for the product. These self-eLearning modules may appear slick and cost-effective, but they will almost never produce an effective result to properly prepare users to be proficient and confident enough when the system goes live. The use of eLearning modules alone will almost certainly result in exceptionally high, long-term Help Desk queries, frustration, and low adoption.

Process Review or Other Kinds of Non-Technical Transformation Projects

All of the same principles are true for non-technical transformation projects, other than the activities required for conducting technical training. Although there is not the same bias of treating training as a 'non-core' project activity, there is often an underestimation of what training, or even *whether* training is required for other kinds of transformation projects. At a minimum, ensure your transformation plan has the following elements:

Assess new-skills needs for every change in a process step or role New skills are required due to new or modified process steps, new tools, new interactions (e.g., direct customer interaction now required where there was none before), or new prerequisite skills (e.g., analytic work now required, where a particular role did not require this before).

Assign Process or Solution Experts equivalent to the Super Users in technical transformations These internal experts will be selected from key functional areas of the business where there are the greatest concentration of stakeholders most affected by the change. As with Super Users, select these experts early, and train and involve them as much as possible in the development and testing of the solution to give them as much advanced knowledge as possible to help support their function with the change.

Work with Human Resources to address changes in organizational roles It's important to ensure that roles significantly impacted by the transformation have a good long-term learning and succession plan in place.

STOP POINT

The Project Manager must look for these warning signs and raise the red STOP flag:

If design time is compressed beyond the point that effective customized materials can be developed If design time is not properly worked into the Project Plan, then the project should stop until executive decision-makers can be convinced adjustments need to be made.

If face-to-face training is not agreed to when obviously needed for good adoption The Project Manager must raise the STOP flag and state that adoption will not occur at an acceptable level if face-to-face training does not occur.

If the right resources are not assigned to the development, delivery, or support of training These activities require special skills. For example, training development specialists typically have a technical writing background for technology transformations. Trainers have facilitation skills, and support resources typically have coaching skills.

My Step 3 Communication Story: Communication Is a Critical Activity!

As the Program Director for a large governmental strategic transformation project, from the very early stages of the project I identified communication as a core project deliverable. One of the first Team Leads hired as part of the Core Project Team was a seasoned Communication Lead. This strategic transformation project involved changing the strategic core business model and processes (divesting major groups of services, and adding and enhancing others), a major restructuring of the entire organization, and a change in both how the organization partnered with external stakeholders and how divisions worked with one another.

In the three years it took to complete the restructuring of the organization's business processes, organizational structure, and job redesign, the project met all deadlines, and relations with the union and employees remained positive as measured by surveys and focus groups. This does not mean that there was no resistance to change or that every group was happy with the change; however, we received a critical mass of support for the consistency and fairness with which the change was implemented. One of the main reasons employees gave for this success was the effectiveness of our planning and managing of project communications. The senior Communication Lead did two things well:

1. She was effective in communicating to and receiving feedback from senior executives and senior managers on communication needs and issues. She was especially effective in creating close relationships and establishing trust with senior leaders.

2. She knew when to communicate the right information, through the right media or channel, to the right audience, in the right language.

Not only the Project Sponsor and I but the entire team knew that our Communication Lead and the whole communication stream were crucial to our project's success. Communication milestones were built into the Critical Path of our integrated project model.

Step 3 Activities: Communication

Most organizations understand or know that communication is important to achieving a successful transformation. In most projects the phrase "no one ever communicated too much on a transformation project" is often stated as a project credo at the outset of a project. And yet, communication is often poorly done and, like training, is treated like the poor cousin of the project. Part of the reason for this is that communication, like training, is often considered support work.

Often, communication is thought of as a 'soft skill.' This creates the perception that these activities are vague and inexact and have mostly to do with the skill of a copywriter. This is not the case. There is a basic set of communication deliverables that should appear in every major project transformation. Without them, there is serious risk of lack of adoption and support, and the building of commitment for the transformation will never occur. If effective communication does not occur at the right time, transformation adoption and commitment will be at risk. Lack of communication creates fear, a lack of trust, and a lack of understanding and initiates a grapevine of inaccurate information that often goes viral.

The communication plan needs to take into consideration a well-researched phenomenon called the Rule of Seven. It is important for transformation leaders to understand it so that they will accept what may seem like a redundant and overly repetitive set of communication activities.

The Advertising Rule of Seven

A common principle often cited in communication plans is that a message needs to be repeated five to seven times before it sticks. This idea seems to come from an old principle from the marketing/advertising world. Most of the marketing and advertising gurus agree that messages need to be repeated more times than you think to stick. However, research shows that other factors, such as consistency of message, the right use of media, and the repetition and appeal of the message, are just as important. You can communicate too much if the message is not a good one or not crafted well.

Create the Project Transformation "Story"

All key elements and context for the project should be developed as a story to be communicated to all key stakeholders. Mostly, these are key elements from the Project Charter, written and presented in a way that is compelling and understandable to the stakeholders, like chapters in a story.

Chapter 1: Create a contextual description of the current state   Set the scene of the current business situation, outlining the organization's overall business and reiterating the strategy, business objectives, priorities, and key challenges.

Chapter 2: Convey the urgency of the need to change within the context just described   Explain why the transformation project is necessary as a key priority project to the organization and why it should be important to all stakeholder groups.

Chapter 3: Describe the solution, emphasizing how it will address this urgent business need   Use non-technical language to describe what is going to be implemented and by when. Provide a clear description of how the solution will solve the urgent need for change for the organization, for each stakeholder function (including external stakeholders, if applicable), and for individuals in key roles.

Chapter 4: State measurable goals in the form of a Transformation Vision   Although sometimes difficult to do, a statement must be created that will clarify what success will look like. It should be impactful and be stated in tangible, measureable terms that stakeholders will understand. What will be different? What will stay the same? What things will no longer occur?

Identify Key Audience Groups

The starting point for creating a communication plan is identifying all stakeholders. Key stakeholders must be identified individually. Other stakeholders should be grouped into their functions, or other groupings should be determined by the need to communicate to them differently.

For example, an IT group needs to know different information than Sales or Finance groups. In a technology transformation where a new system is being introduced, an IT Help Desk needs to know different information than an IT development or architecture group.

Maintain the stakeholder list throughout the project. Develop ways to keep it current, perhaps tapping into the organization's Human Resource Information System.

Create Key Project Messages

Key project messages are the messages that the project will repeat over and over to help create and increase awareness throughout the project. It typically and most effectively will be the most positive and impactful elements of the transformation, crafted in simple statements that can be used in presentations and as branded statements in project written materials.

Develop a Set of Communication Guiding Principles

It is important that the Project Team develop a set of communication guiding principles that it will live by, which will be championed by the Project Manager and monitored by every Project Team member. The purpose of developing these guiding principles is to gain Project Team commitment for presenting a consistent and believable stream of communication throughout the project and to help stakeholders develop trust and confidence in the project transformation solution.

Guiding principles for communication developed by other effective Transformation Teams include that the communication be:

Timely Messages are delivered at the right time in the most expedient way. This includes that meetings should start and finish on time and attendees should ensure they arrive on time to avoid inconveniencing others.

Structured and well planned   Communication events should have a structure that is clear to all recipients/attendees.

Purposeful   If a communication event does not have a clear purpose, then the Team should question whether the event should continue.

Honest and frank   Communication events should be open and truthful. Deliberate, destructive, and/or misleading communication should be avoided.

Simple   Messages need to be simple and easy to follow.

Specific   Messages need to be specific as to the purpose of the event. Vagueness or innuendo should be avoided.

Consistent   The communication products/events must send a consistent message that builds on previous communication.

Conforming   Messages and communication products must conform to company corporate standards.

The Project Manager should present examples of communication guiding principles to the Project Team and develop a consensual list of principles that the Team can believe in and promote throughout the life of the project. The Project Manager or any other Project Team member should use principles both to help them communicate in their ongoing project work and to challenge anyone who believes the principles are not being adhered to.

Develop a Communication Schedule

Develop a detailed communication schedule spreadsheet that lists all key information that needs to be delivered. Elements that should appear on the plan include:

- communication activity or event
- stakeholder individual(s) and/or groups that need to receive the communication
- date(s) of communication (single or regular intervals)
- content objective and summary objectives
- content developer
- message deliverer
- communication channel and/or media
- feedback mechanism

This communication plan will appear as part of the overall plan and will be managed by whoever is accountable for the communication stream (either the Project Manager or a Communication Specialist). It is highly recommended that an internal Communication Specialist be assigned as the lead on this role. The Communication Specialist typically understands the current organizational media, channels, and audiences and will be a quicker study and a more cost-effective choice than an external advisor. However, there is often value in hiring external Communication Specialists who have experience in implementing similar transformations and also know what works well in the same or related business sectors.

Communicate the Communication Plan

Create a single-page calendar view of your transformation communication plan that you will continually update to 'communicate the communication plan.' This view will be presented at Steering Committee meetings and functional group updates to continually let people know that you have a rich and constant flow of communication about the project that is being implemented and managed.

Develop Frequently Asked Questions

An effective and efficient communication document is Frequently Asked Questions (commonly known as FAQs). FAQs are categorized answers to questions that typically get asked over and over by stakeholders. The objectives of FAQs are to:

Publish an easily accessible document Start by placing the "transformation story" in an easily accessible electronic location, such as the company website. It should provide all employees with a clear understanding of the change—typically covering the 5 Ws: the what, why, who, when, and where of the change. Keep the document up to date, and enrich the information as appropriate and required over the course of the transformation.

Create consistent language for the transformation   One of the principles cited in this section is that messaging be frequent *and* consistent. The more people hear the same message over and over, the more they will remember it. In one project assignment, stakeholders were commenting that they were receiving mixed messages from the Project Team. In reality, different Project Team Leads were creating their own presentation decks and paraphrasing high-level messages in their own words. The content wasn't really different in most cases, but people were confused. The Project Manager reacted by stating that all formal presentations to stakeholders had to be reviewed by the Project Communication Lead. Over time, Project Team Leads learned to consult FAQs and other formal documents to repeat language.

Initially, ask and answer questions that best describe key elements of the project that the Team wants to communicate   The Communication Lead of the Project Team should create these questions about the transformation project. As communication sessions and Stakeholder Readiness work takes place, more questions will arise that can be added to FAQs. Judgment should be used to include only those FAQs that will have long-term relevance.

Develop and Maintain a Glossary
Communication should be as free of jargon, acronyms, and technical terms as possible. Every organization has its

communication culture, which has often become so natural to long-term employees that they don't realize they have created a different language. This unique 'language' can occur on an organizational level and within certain functions. At an organizational level, this may not be a problem, if all stakeholders know and practise this unique language. However, for technology transformations, the project is usually managed and communicated from the IT function, and the language used is often too technical for the rest of the organization to understand. Every effort should be made to use simple business language.

Often, the project cannot totally avoid technical or other new terms when communicating the transformation. If the project is a technology transformation, stakeholders must understand the product names and terms used in the system itself. New concepts may have common industry terms that must be used to educate stakeholders. Therefore, it is useful to create a glossary that will be maintained, updated, and made easily accessible to the Project Team and all stakeholders, similar to the FAQs.[2]

Use Shared-Document Software

It is critical that documents have strict version control and easy access for the Team and other key stakeholders. Many teams use document-sharing software such as SharePoint,

---

2   A glossary is included at the end of this book to practise what is being preached. Although jargon is largely avoided, there are concepts and terms commonly used in transformation projects that the author wants Project Managers to be aware of and that are helpful in Community of Practice discussions.

which helps address both of these issues. Typically, the Project Coordinator organizes and manages the entire site, but Team Leads manage their own data areas. Other stakeholders in the organization can be given access to relevant documents.

Create and Maintain Feedback Mechanisms

For every communication activity and document delivered to a stakeholder audience, the Project Manager should ensure there is a way that the audience can ask questions, raise concerns, or make suggestions ... and that a response is provided in a reasonable period of time. Throughout the implementation of the transformation project, the Project Manager and Team should be looking for ways to get stakeholders engaged and involved. 'Telling' doesn't create support and commitment, no matter how compelling the message is. Every time stakeholders communicate back to the Project Team, it should be viewed as an opportunity to start a conversation and engage and involve them.

Develop Communication Lead–Project Sponsor Rapport

All high-performing and effective Communication Leads I have met had one thing in common: they were very good at establishing and maintaining a good rapport with the Project Sponsor. A Project Sponsor must be seen as the active lead of the project and an effective communicator to all stakeholders on an individual, group, and entire organizational level. Good Communication Leads can coach and guide Project Sponsors in what and when they should communicate and through which media. I have even seen experienced Communication

Leads coach senior Project Sponsors in their major presentations to senior executives and large groups for key milestone messages.

CHAPTER 4

Step 4: Launch the Transformation Project

Stop talking. Start walking.

—L.M. Heroux

My Step 4 Story: Bad Launch / Good Launch

Scenario 1: I once had the role of Change Management Lead in a large enterprise technology project that had been launched several months before I came on board. No real change management resources or change management activities had been planned or executed, so I was in catch-up mode from the start. The first thing I noticed in the first Project Team meeting I attended was a feeling of disconnection among Team members. Key members were missing from the meeting, and when I asked where they were, I was told that some never attend the Team meetings because "they are in another building." I was surprised that some Team members in the room didn't seem to know one another that well—two of them being introduced to each other at the same time I was introduced. After the meeting I asked whether they were also new Team members like me. I was told that one had been with the Team three weeks, and the other eight weeks.

I met with the Project Team Lead after the meeting and asked him how this project was launched and how Team members kept in touch. He stated that the Team didn't really have a formal launch because only a few members started doing all the work, and members joined at different times. Team Leads were supposed to attend project meetings weekly, but he had been having trouble getting some of them to attend because of other conflicting meetings and the inconvenience of location. Some Team Leads also complained that Team meetings took away too much time from getting their work done, so they just didn't attend. In addition, every month he held a full team meeting for all Team members to attend to get an idea of status.

I was flabbergasted at the lack of teamwork I was observing. I asked him what he thought of the Team's performance as a cohesive unit. He told me frankly that it was poor and asked for suggestions. We began putting a plan in place to establish better Team communications, but we had a long road ahead of us to make the changes. We lost a few Team members along the way and missed a few deadlines because of poor productivity before things started to improve.

Scenario 2: Several years ago, I worked with a colleague as the Senior Change Management Lead for a major technology transformation project. We were hired as part of the initial Core

Project Team and worked together with the Project Manager and Project Sponsor to strategize on an effective change management plan. One of the key activities my colleague and I recommended to the Project Manager and Project Sponsor was to deliver a full-day Project Launch session as soon as all Core Team members were assigned or hired. They both agreed, and together we designed and supported delivery of a full-day Team Project Launch session. The session included:

- introductory exercises where Team members got to know one another personally and professionally

- presentations from the Project Sponsor and Project Manager on the full scope of the project, schedule milestones, project challenges, risks, Project Governance, and roles and responsibilities

- presentations by each Team Lead that they had prepared to give the full Team a good understanding of their project work stream, what their deliverables were, who they needed to work with on the Project Team, and how they would be interacting with stakeholders

- a Team exercise to get people to open up a bit, share experiences, and have a little fun

- lots of time for questions and answers

- a promise at the end of the session to keep the Team informed and involved and to maintain good feedback channels for all to pose their questions, concerns, and suggestions

The beginning of the day started with a lot of tentative and even worried faces around the room. When we finished the day, we could all feel the energy. Feedback from the session included comments from individuals who thanked us for making them understand the project and their role and, most importantly, making each of them feel like a valued member of the Team. My colleague and I believed we were successful in jet-starting the Team toward becoming a high-performing team.

Step 4 Activities

Once there is true executive understanding and commitment to the project solution and an established journey to achieve it, it is time to formally launch the transformation project. It is critical to create understanding, accountability, energy, excitement, and a good foundation in order to develop a high-performing team. The following are some key activities that each Project Manager of a major transformation project needs to include in launching the project.

Assign or Hire Other Specialist Resources

At this point, the Project Manager should have a resource-loaded Project Plan, with input from key stakeholders and Core Team Leads now assigned to the project. It is time to assign or hire the full Project Team required to deliver all aspects of the approved plan, including those with technical, administrative, and other specialized skills.

Ideally, the Project Manager and relevant Team Lead should meet individually with each member as soon as they begin, to ensure they understand their role in relation to the Project Charter and overall transition.

Conduct a Project Launch Team Session

As soon as the full Project Team has been assigned and all members are ready to begin, the Project Manager should create and conduct a comprehensive Project Launch session, inviting all Team members. There are several objectives of a Project Launch session:

- to create a common understanding of the purpose and importance of the transformation project
- for each Team member to understand the value of their contribution to the overall goals of the project
- for each Team member to understand all Team functions, roles, and dependencies
- to openly share information, including challenges, risks, and initial issues that the Project Team needs to address
- to encourage questions and discussions to help establish a culture of openness and transparency
- to create positive energy and urgency

Ideally, the session will last a full day and be held away from the project office. If this is not possible, at least gain agreement from leadership and participants that the session will be undisturbed by normal workday interruptions.

TYPICAL AGENDA

The Project Sponsor should introduce the session, stating commitment to the project and accountability for ensuring that the Team has continuous organizational and executive support throughout the life of the project. Here is a typical agenda:

1. Begin with informal introductions—some icebreakers—for the Team to get to know one another.

2. The Project Manager does a project overview, reviewing at a minimum:

   a. the organizational imperative of implementing this transformation

   b. major elements of the Project Charter

   c. Project Governance

   d. internal Team and external organization communication

   e. individual Team accountabilities

3. Each Project Team Lead gives a more specific presentation of what work needs to be accomplished.

4. Conduct a Team activity to get Team members to interact and experience different communication styles. Use exercises that allow Team members to get to know one another either one-on-one or in small groups.

5. Conduct group/Team discussion on project risks, questions, and concerns. (Use these questions as a starting point for ongoing weekly discussions.)

6. Ensure all Team members have one another's full contact information as well as that for other organizational contacts they will need.

7. Announce the next Project Team meeting.

8. The Project Manager ends the meeting by stating how he or she intends to keep the Team connected.

Communicate the Launch of the Project Team

Immediately after the Project Launch, an appropriate communication should be released to all employees who will eventually be affected by the change. Typically, a short communication would go out to all employees, and face-to-face meetings should be conducted with groups of employees affected more directly. Topics to be covered in the face-to-face meetings include:

- Why is the company spending time and money on this project?

- What is hoped to be accomplished (in measurable, tangible terms) and by when?

- What will change for the organization? For individual employees?

- What are the next steps?

- How will the Project Team be communicating to employees throughout the preparation, launch, and post-launch support period of the transformation project to let them know how things are going?

- How can employees contact the Project Team if they have any questions, comments, or suggestions?

CHAPTER 5

Step 5: Build a High-Performing Transformation Project Team

I don't believe in team motivation. I believe in getting a team prepared so it knows it will have the necessary confidence when it steps on a field and be prepared to play a good game.
　　　　　　　　　　　　　—Tom Landry

My Step 5 Story: Why Did Every Project Manager Want to Work for Michael?

Several years ago I worked on a government project as a Program Manager of a substantial strategic transformation for a large Canadian provincial ministry. The executive level stakeholders were a group of Assistant Deputy Ministers, including one I worked with quite closely early in the project (whom I will call Michael). Besides learning that he was a great person to work with, I learned that employees who worked in his division really liked working for him ... especially those who worked directly for him. I assumed it was just because he was a really nice guy and easy to work with.

Eventually I learned why employees were so loyal to Michael. One of the sub-projects I was managing as part of the overall transformation program was to create a ministry-wide Project Management Office. The first step I took was to interview senior executives within the ministry who had major accountability for managing large, high-priority, multi-functional Project Teams. Michael was one of the first I interviewed because he managed more formal projects than any other executive in the ministry. When I asked him his philosophy on managing projects, he told me: "I try to create a positive project management culture by telling Project Managers who work for me: 'I will always thank you for telling me that any element of your project is "yellow," but I will not be very happy when a project suddenly goes from green to red.' In other words, I want problems to be raised in real time." I talked to some of his people, and they all said similar things: "Michael is great. He often praises our teams publicly for bringing issues or risks to the attention of the leadership very early ... these yellow flags are almost treated as wins. Consequently, we are always diligently looking for these issues and risks, and we are proud of our project management success record." Consequently, Project Managers and other employees who worked for Michael were very motivated, went that extra mile to produce results, and generally had very good project results.

Step 5 Activities

Most organizations understand that it is important to develop a high-performing team in order to deliver project results efficiently and effectively. However, such teams are rare, mainly because people don't understand what they are. The following outlines how to set the stage for quickly building and maintaining a high-performing Project Team.

What Does a High-Performing Team Look Like?

A model that has been around for years argues that Teams may go through four phases of development, though many get stuck for too long in the early phases and do not reach the latter. This model has proven accurate and useful for Project Leaders and their Teams. In order to create a high-performing Team, a Project Manager needs to understand what a Team looks like at each stage.

TEAM DEVELOPMENT PHASE	DESCRIPTION	PRODUCTIVITY LEVEL
Forming	When Teams first get together, they are unsure of their roles, how to interact with the Team, and how to get things done co-operatively. Team members look to leaders for direction, and work activities are usually completed more slowly than required. Good clarity of roles, strong leadership, and good governance can move the Team quickly through this first phase of development.	Low
Storming	Team members get to know one another better, and begin challenging both one another and the leadership. New Team members have to get used to working differently and must go through their own change	Very Low

⮕

TEAM DEVELOPMENT PHASE	DESCRIPTION	PRODUCTIVITY LEVEL
	process. Arguments may ensue and productivity may drop with Team members working at cross-purposes as they try to establish themselves and their norms in the Team. Teams may get stuck in this mode or even fail if Storming becomes too severe. The Project Team Lead needs to recognize early signs of Storming and work with Project Team members, both individually and as a Team, to quickly help the Team work well together.	
Norming	At some point, a Project Team will learn to interact more effectively, as Team members understand and learn to accept one another's different roles and styles. The Norming phase is characterized by Team members communicating more effectively and dealing with issues on their own. Productivity will rise as Team members take the time to work through and resolve these issues. Roles are more fully understood and accepted. Many Project Teams reach this level of Project Team performance and stay there. Often, organizations believe Teams that reach this stage are high-performing teams. Although the Project Team might appear to be getting along well, a good Project Manager/Leader will recognize that productivity is still not optimum, returning only mediocre or barely acceptable results.	Mediocre
Performing	Only a small number of Project Teams will reach the state of a high-performing team. The best way to recognize such a Team is to observe it completing a task that requires coordination from multiple members. Observers would have trouble following workflow and how tasks get done, but things would seem to get done quickly and effectively, with seemingly little communication on task. For those readers who are hockey fans, it's similar to watching hockey legend Wayne Gretzky pass without looking to a teammate on the famed Edmonton Oilers in their heyday. How did he do that? Apart from Gretzky's greatness, it is the result of continuous practice as a team and understanding exactly where each player needs to be, what each player needs	High

TEAM DEVELOPMENT PHASE	DESCRIPTION	PRODUCTIVITY LEVEL
	to do, and when, in any situation. A high-performing team is like that. It focuses on perfecting the delivery of coordinated Team tasks. A good Project Team Lead is one who recognizes that a Team is ready to start performing at a higher level and then coaches Team members to practise the important tasks as a team over and over until they are perfect (no errors, high quality, and high speed).	

Team development through the phases is both non-linear and unstable. It is non-linear because Team performance does not progress in a straight line—it normally gets worse or moves up and down before becoming truly effective. It is unstable because once performance has achieved a certain level, it may stay where it is or move backward or forward. It might move backward if a new Team member enters the mix or if project issues arise that affect individual Team members' roles. Understanding that Team performance has to be managed and worked on throughout the life of the project, the Project Manager must constantly look for signs of changes that need to be addressed.

Apply Best Practices and Principles to Create a High-Performing Team

CO-LOCATE

Teamwork is greatly enhanced when the Team works together in the same workspace. Members get to know one another and can resolve issues and address problems in real time. Face-to-face discussion greatly decreases misunderstandings that often occur on the phone or via email. Virtual teams are possible but often fail. From a team development perspective, your Team is at a great disadvantage if it is not co-located.

However, there are situations where it is impossible to co-locate all the Team members, for example, in a large organization with multiple locations. If one or two members need to work remotely, consider the following ways to keep them connected:

- Use videoconferencing wherever possible for meetings and key work activities.

- Have them visit for milestone meetings or presentations.

- Visit them or have other Team members visit them.

- Have more frequent phone conversations with them to check for understanding, probe for issues, and listen; encourage other Team members to do the same.

- Make it your business to understand the operations and key stakeholders in the outside location.

MAKE WEEKLY MEETINGS MEANINGFUL

Discussion at weekly meetings should focus on areas that are yellow or red; review project risks or issues; introduce new information or concepts; or educate the Team.

Weekly project meetings should NOT simply review the status of all project tasks for each Functional Team. Project Managers often do this, but it has no purpose or relevance for all Team Leads/members in the room. It is expensive to have everyone in a meeting room, so ensure there is a valuable purpose for doing so.

One technique that works well is to give every Team member permission to question what the meeting objectives are and why their role and attendance is required. I have worked with more than one Project Manager who has told the Team: "If the meeting organizer cannot give you a meeting objective and why you are attending, you have my permission to inform them you will not attend."

CONDUCT BRIEF, IMMEDIATE-RESPONSE DAILY MEETINGS

It is very valuable for small Project Teams, or each Functional Team, to meet every day for ten to fifteen minutes. These quick 'team huddles' should be facilitated by the Project Manager or Team Lead (depending on the Team makeup) as a way for each Team member to identify specific barriers that prevent them from getting work done and as a way to stay on top of any other issues.

No problem solving should occur in these brief meetings. The Project Manager or Team Lead should follow up on any issues after the meeting.

CREATE AN ATMOSPHERE OF OPENNESS AND FRANKNESS

The opening story about the Assistant Deputy Minister I named Michael characterized how senior leaders can create a healthy atmosphere of openness and frankness in their Project Teams. Besides following the example in the story, there are a few good principles for Project Managers to live by to create this culture:

Encourage Team members to speak up Do this by not allowing criticism of suggestions or concerns in open Team discussions. Team members will not offer their early concerns, issues, or suggestions if they think they will get shot down because the idea is either not popular or not yet thought through or analyzed.

ositively reinforce yellow flags   Welcoming the input of Team members who raise a concern or list their work stream as yellow gets everyone in the mode of looking for problems or issues.

Communicate issues to the Team in real time   You never know where solutions will come from. Team members also feel more trusted and involved when they know what is going on in the project.

KEEP THE SPONSOR VISIBLE AND ACCESSIBLE

Scenario 1:   There was one senior Project Sponsor (in a major financial institution) who worked on the same floor as the Core Project Team she sponsored. Most of the Team were internal Team members, and most reported through other managers to her. Her office was located on the other side of the floor, tucked away in a corner where no one could see her. When she came to the office, she made a beeline from the elevator to her office. When she had meetings, she walked straight to the elevators to get to her meeting. In a given month, one hand was more than enough to count the number of visits by this executive to her Project Team. Granted, she was vastly overworked and understaffed, but when asked to become more visible to her Project Team and other key stakeholders, she replied, "That is not my job. That is why I have a Project Manager." In addition, the Project Manager was an external consultant. This lack of visibility and of 'connectedness' between the Project Team and the Sponsor and leadership resulted in a number of Team development challenges, including lack of trust, lack of feeling valued, a sense of impending project disaster (aided by a rampant grapevine), and a general feeling of not being part of a supported, organization-wide endeavour.

In fairness to this individual, abdication really occurred at a higher level early in the project. It was not really fair that she was given the active sponsorship role: she was not the ideal person, and she did not have the capacity to deliver what was needed. The Executive Team did not do their due diligence on gaining executive buy-in and on capacity planning. Although the above example is an extreme, it is not an uncommon example of how Project Sponsors delegate or 'abdicate' their responsibility as active sponsors for major project transformations.

Scenario 2: Another Project Sponsor client I worked for had an entirely different way of interacting with her group. She constantly met individually with each of the Team Leads and frequently visited different work areas of her very large Project Team. She got intimately involved in every major issue and risk discussion, inviting all Team members who could contribute to the discussion into meetings to brainstorm solutions. Many Project Managers may consider this method of management 'over-managing'; I considered it as positive, active project sponsorship. This Project Sponsor's style of interacting resulted in her Team feeling valued, involved, and motivated to solve problems quickly. In addition, the Project Sponsor was prepared to discuss risks and issues confidently with executive stakeholders, with first-hand knowledge and insight.

These examples, and many other situations I have experienced throughout my career, prove that the Project Sponsor should be visible to the Team throughout the preparation, launch, and support of the transformation, occasionally attending Team meetings and walking around to talk to Team members. The Sponsor should know the name of EVERY Team member and demonstrate he or she knows and values their contribution.

The Sponsor should participate in every major Team communication event. They typically would open proceedings, provide organizational context for project context, and spend some time listening to Team issues and ideas.

If Project Managers notice that this is not occurring, they must raise it as a concern with the Project Sponsor. Every mainstream change management methodology out there agrees on one basic thing:

> The number-one cause of failure in major transformation projects is the lack of active and effective project sponsorship.

USE THE PROJECT MANAGER'S TIME FOR 'WALK-ABOUTS' AND 'TALK-ABOUTS'

The Project Sponsor needs to be visible to the Team, perhaps via minimum weekly visits. However, the Project Manager should be continually walking around, connecting with the Team. If possible, the Project Manager should walk into every Project Team workspace at least once a day, even just to say, "Hello, how are things going?"

One technique I am a big advocate of is daily, very brief meetings with immediate reports. Project Managers can do this with their Team Leads, and Team Leads can to it with each of their project work groups. This daily meeting would last no more than ten to fifteen minutes. Its main purpose is to quickly verify what work each Team member is working on and what new issues or challenges have arisen that day.

No problem solving would occur during this quick meeting, but the Team Leader would follow up immediately after the meeting with any Team member who raised an issue, to see what he or she could do to help sort out the issue or challenge.

It is easy to see that if Project Managers used this approach, they would be spending a great amount of time simply connecting with their Team and helping them fix problems. I presented this concept once to a group of very experienced Project Managers, and one made the comment, "If I did what you are suggesting, then I would never get any work done!" My response? "That is your work. There is nothing more important you could do as a Project Manager than continuously spending your time talking to your Team and removing issues and barriers to their work. Their job is to get work tasks and deliverables completed. Your job is to help them do it ... that is what managing your project is."

Another key relationship is between the Project Manager and the Project Sponsor. The Project Manager should have full daily informal access and should formally meet at least weekly with the Project Sponsor to:

- review the status of the project and overall risks

- resolve internal Team issues

- strategize on lack of commitment and support from executives or other key stakeholders

- prepare for the next Steering Committee presentation

- develop appropriate Sponsor activities for the project

Conduct Occasional Project Integration Sessions

Shortly after the Project Launch, the Project Manager should conduct the first Project Integration Session. Its main purpose is to validate the dependencies of the project with all key Functional Leads and required specialists and experts.

Team Leads should prepare individual presentations to describe each element of their section of the work plan. They should include an explanation of:

- each Work Package (major group of tasks) so that the whole Team understands what the work is, who is doing it, and why it is important

- all dependencies required for each of these Work Packages (what work needs to be accomplished before each of these Work Packages can be worked on)

- what each Work Package is a dependency for (what other work is depending upon each respective Work Package)

- any risks, issues, or questions (e.g., unknown information) related to each Work Package

The Project Manager facilitates this session with the overarching purpose of:

- identifying the project Critical Path (the Project Manager should have this prepared before the meeting)

- obtaining full Team understanding of how their deliverables fit into the overall Project Plan—most importantly, ensuring each Team Lead and specialist understands the flow of work and who is depending upon their work to be done and by when

This is the key meeting on beginning to figure out how the full Team works together.

A war-room approach often works well for complex projects with a lot of interdependencies. If a Project Room can be dedicated to the Team, the Critical Path and dependencies can be left up for the whole Team to see and have engrained in their minds as to when work needs to be completed, status, dependencies, and key status updates.

NOTE: Chapter 8 (Manage the Transformation—Reset the Project Plan at Milestones or Gates) includes a more complete discussion on how to conduct a Project Integration Session.

HAVE A MONTHLY SOCIAL EVENT

Informal get-togethers work really well to develop team spirit, infuse positive energy, and bring the Team closer. These could be lunches, evening gatherings, or whatever works well for the Team. Perhaps rotate the timing and type of event to accommodate everyone. Let the Team decide and organize these.

CHAPTER 6

Step 6: Assess the Degree of Support and Resistance for the Transformation Project

I alone cannot change the world, but I can cast a stone across the waters to create many ripples.

—Mother Teresa

My Step 7 Story: Why It Is So Hard to Get an Accurate Employee List?

Early in my role as the Change Management Lead for a major strategic transformation in the government sector, I had my first argument with the Project Manager and project leadership. The transformation involved totally redefining the organization's business model, which would result in changing business functions, major reorganization, and job redesign.

I requested that the Project Team and Human Resources support me in identifying every major stakeholder who would be affected by this change. I met with immediate resistance:

From the Project Team: "This exercise will take too much time and does not all have to be done at this very early stage of the project. We will uncover who all the stakeholders impacted by changes are as we redesign each division's organizational structure and roles. Besides, we are too burdened with a lack of resources and need to meet deadlines for us to meet your request."

From Human Resources: "It may sound like an easy task to get accurate employee lists and organizational charts, but it is actually quite a challenge. Our Human Resource Information System (HRIS) is accurate for compensation purposes, but we have had challenges keeping role and organizational chart information accurate and up-to-date. It would be a monumental task to get this information quickly, and frankly, we don't have the resources to do it."

I immediately raised these objections as an issue that needed to be resolved immediately if the Change Management plan was to succeed. We had a meeting and I posed my argument to the Project Sponsor:

This is a major transformation project whose success hinges on developing effective organizational solutions that need to conform to a new business model, which will deeply affect many employees and their roles. We need to get an accurate picture of everyone who is affected so we can begin engaging with them to both communicate what this project is about and how and when we think they will be impacted. As soon as we announce our intentions, we will create fear among all employees. If we keep some of them in the dark, they will fear the worst. We need to gain control of these discussions from the outset. The knowledge we will get from engaging with all stakeholders early will help inform our solution and our schedule. Finally, without an accurate listing of all employees' formal roles, we run the risk of designing ineffective or inaccurate solutions. We need to begin our project with a comprehensive stakeholder map, listing all employees who will be impacted by the change and the organizational structure.

Luckily, the Project Sponsor agreed with me, since he had experience running other major transformations. We created an accurate stakeholder map, and it paid dividends immediately because it was different than the existing map. As Human Resources had warned us, their records hadn't kept up with some significant organizational structure and role changes that Divisional Leaders had put in place in the past few years. This information considerably changed both the strategy on the solution design and the overall project implementation schedule. I immediately began engaging with individuals and functional groups to determine and categorize support and resistance for the change.

Without the creation of an accurate and comprehensive stakeholder map, our Project Team would have been operating in the dark.

Step 6 Activities

The first five steps of the 10-Step change methodology are all about getting executive support and setting up the project for success. Step 6 is where the real change management work of the transformation project begins. The Project Manager must create a baseline measurement that shows what level of support and readiness exists within the organization before devising a change plan.

Dispelling Some Misconceptions

Before outlining the assessment activities, it is important to understand four myths that exist about managing change in an organization.

MYTH #1: EVERYONE MUST CHANGE

It is unrealistic for any organization to believe that they will be able to achieve full adoption and commitment to the change across all stakeholder groups. Not everyone will adapt well to the change or support it. A graph showing where positive support and where resistance exist among all stakeholders can be found in Figure 4.

This curve shows that the bulk of stakeholders are neutral on the change. A minority are either resistant/very negative or very positive. The natural reaction of most Transformation Project Leaders is to focus on working on the vocal negative minority. My experience is that it is not worth the time and energy trying to get the minority on board (unless they are a key senior stakeholder). The best strategy is to focus on the large group in the middle and just to the left of the neutral point.

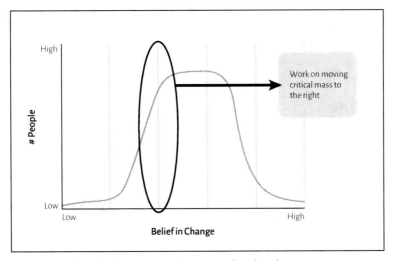

FIGURE 4. Distribution curve of support for the change among stakeholders

The idea is to move enough of these individuals to create a 'tipping point.'[1] If you succeed, the whole curve will naturally move to the right.

Spend as little time as possible with the negative detractors of the transformation project, unless they are disruptive to your project efforts. Stakeholders who are at the most negative point of the graph will either move or be left behind and become less relevant to your change.

---

1 "The Tipping Point is defined as the moment of critical mass, the threshold, and the boiling point. It is the point when everyday things reach epidemic proportions. There are three distinct characteristics of epidemics—contagiousness, the fact that little causes can have big effects, and that change happens not gradually but at one dramatic moment." The three characteristics are: Law of the Few, the Sticking Factor, and the Power of Context. Malcolm Gladwell, *The Tipping Point* (New York: Back Bay Books, 2002). Excerpt from: http://faculty.darden.virginia.edu/GBUS885-00/Student_Reviews/Antoine.htm.

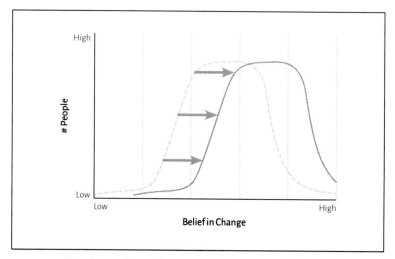

FIGURE 5. Tipping point effect moves the distribution curve of support in a positive direction

MYTH #2: YOU CAN MAKE PEOPLE CHANGE

There is a widespread belief that good leaders can make people change and 'see the light.' The truth is that many years of behavioural research show that motivation comes from within. The best we can do as leaders is influence people in making them want to change themselves. There is a big difference in these two approaches. Some leaders believe if they repeat a message enough or tell people they must act a certain way, people will change. Authoritative figures might be able to coerce people to follow the new rules, but they cannot force commitment. And only true commitment will guarantee maximum effort and optimum results. Leaders who subscribe to this latter philosophy understand that they must find out what will motivate individuals to want to support the change of their own volition.

Daryl Conner is a Change Management guru. Conner identifies multiple stages of commitment that people must experience before they internalize and are committed to the change affecting them. His model shows that real support for change can be a lengthy and complex process that can also be derailed.[2]

MYTH #3: EVERYONE WILL UNDERSTAND THE RATIONALE FOR CHANGE

One view that often creates a blind spot for leaders trying to implement big changes in their organization is a belief that everyone will see things the way that they do. Leaders have told me: "How can people disagree with the facts and story we are presenting to them? It's just common sense."

When I begin a new project, I always start by telling the Sponsor and all key Team members: "When it comes to understanding and developing commitment to the change, it is unimportant and, indeed, irrelevant what you think. We need to figure out what everyone else thinks." This has become my mantra to my Project Team members in any major transformation:

> When it comes to change, people will not perceive the change the same way ... there is no common sense.

What may seem to you to be a perfectly reasonable case for change may seem completely unreasonable to others. For example, you may be introducing a new state-of-the-art system that will make things more effective and easier to use. You will also be training people to be much more skilled and,

---

2   www.connerpartners.com/blog-posts-containing-downloadable-tools/
    the-eight-stages-of-building-commitment

ultimately, more marketable both within the organization and in the marketplace. Why would anyone disagree with this common sense rationale? One group of employees is listening to this presentation, and although they hear the words being spoken, a number of them are skeptical, and many feel resistant. The reasons for these stakeholders filtering the message differently could be:

- They know the current system well and haven't had to learn anything new in years. They may fear they won't be as skilled in this new system and will be at risk in their 'new job.'

- They have read how a lot of these systems have failed and life was miserable for users as they adjusted to a new cumbersome system.

- They are nervous this new system will eliminate jobs or eliminate aspects of their jobs that they like.

The key to understanding this reality is that the Project Manager or Leader first understands that no matter how compelling a message is, everyone filters messages differently. The Project Manager's/Leader's job is to find out how people have filtered these messages, organize that information into a baseline set of data, and then develop a plan to address concerns and fears.

MYTH #4: THE CHANGE SOLUTION WILL BE GOOD FOR EVERYONE

Although the change will have passed initial scrutiny by all affected functional executives as beneficial for the whole organization, it may not directly benefit all stakeholders. Perhaps it will be more difficult in the short or even longer term for groups of employees. It might even be more difficult and even undesirable for some groups of employees. There is nothing more maddening for employees than to hear how great the transformation will be for the whole organization and then realize that things might actually be worse for them.

For instance, when ERP systems are introduced, many executives are excited by the new depth and accuracy of reporting potentially at their disposal. However, there will undoubtedly be pockets of individuals who will not be as happy about the change. Some users may lose functionality or not be required to do some analytical tasks that they enjoyed and have become expert at performing.

BE HONEST when addressing employees. Your goal is not to dress up the change to make it sound appealing to everyone. Your goal is (1) to be clear about the benefits and necessity of making these changes if the organization is to be successful and (2) to accurately describe what the changes will be to employees' work or jobs, recognizing that many may see benefits, some may not experience benefits or even much change, and some may experience a negative effect.

A lot of my colleagues who help manage change are very good with communicating the benefits and necessity of change—point (1) above. However, I have often debated with colleagues and clients on point (2). Many believe that you have to look hard for, and sometimes even 'spin,' the positive WIIFMs (what's in it for me) for all affected stakeholders. I am convinced this is the wrong approach. People will see through messages that are disingenuous. However, the way to temper a message that may be unwelcome is to describe how individuals will be supported through the change and thank stakeholders in advance for helping to implement a change that may be difficult for them.

Create a Comprehensive Assessment of Resistance and Support

Gather information on statements of resistance and support, where it comes from, and the context for that resistance and support. Use a template that allows you to easily assess what benefits have been positively received and to gain understanding of where resistance lies, why it is there, and how widespread it is.

SPONSOR MEETS STEERING COMMITTEE MEMBERS INDIVIDUALLY

It is important for the Sponsor to open and maintain a dialogue with each executive, continually assessing his or her level of support. Although a Project Charter will have been signed and individual meetings will have already occurred with each Executive Steering Committee member, it is now time to focus on developing true individual support for the life of the project.

Discussion Items

1. Ask each Executive Steering Committee member what their main business objectives and priorities are (individually and by function). Discuss how the transformation project will positively enhance one or more of these objectives.

2. Discuss short-term pain frankly (learning and ramp-up time, initial cost, resource time required by this area) and

be prepared to identify what the short-term pain is. The less surprise, the more support.

3. Determine individual risks, issues, or concerns that the Executive Steering Committee has. Work together on a plan to address each of these concerns.

4. Determine an appropriate venue for the Project Team to present face-to-face to the Executive Steering Committee, both initially and ongoing.

NOTE: If the Project Sponsor and Project Manager judge that the executive stakeholder has any serious issue or reservation with the solution, then the issue should be resolved with a consensual plan of action before addressing that executive's Functional Team.

SPONSOR AND/OR PROJECT MANAGER MEETS FUNCTIONAL TEAMS

A good next step is for the Project Sponsor and Project Manager to meet separately with each major business functional group that is most impacted by the change. Invite other Core Team Leads or members who can contribute to the meeting discussion.

AGENDA ITEMS

1. Introduce the project. The executive leaders (not the Project Sponsor or Project Manager) should kick off this first meeting for the sole purpose of demonstrating support for the project to his/her group. Functional leaders and employees of the function must see that the transformation project is an organizationally driven project, not a Project Team–driven project.

2. Introduce key members of the Project Team (at minimum, the Project Lead, all Team Leads, and key specialists). A good rule of thumb is to have in attendance all Project Team members who may potentially have to communicate and/or work with this functional group of employees.

3. The Project Sponsor and Project Manager review critical topics. It is good practice for the Project Sponsor to present the high-level need and vision for the transformation project, and the Project Manager to cover off details, such as:

   - Why the project is essential for the organization

   - What measurable results the project is hoping to achieve (and by when)

   - How the transformation will help both the organization and this Functional Team achieve/improve its measurable results, or the way work gets done

   - How, and when, the Functional Team (and individual roles) will be affected:

     ◊ What will change (technology, process, and people)

     ◊ What will stay the same

     ◊ What work/activities will be new and what will no longer be required

   - How and when employees will be trained before and supported after launch

   - How employees on the Functional Team will need to be involved during the Project Team's work in preparation for launch

- How the Project Team will communicate with employees in the executive's function: present a communication schedule, feedback mechanisms, and contact information

4. Facilitate a discussion to find out:

- What elements of the transformation these 'internal customers' value

- What elements of the transformation create concern or are disliked

- What the expectations are for how the project is run and what the transformation product and/or service should look like

- What the current business culture of the organization is, and how the change will affect that current culture[3]

CONDUCT A STAKEHOLDER READINESS ANALYSIS

After the Project Team has presented to each functional internal-customer area, the Project Manager needs to conduct a Stakeholder Readiness analysis. The purpose of a Stakeholder Readiness analysis is:

- to understand what impact the transformation solution will have on each group of stakeholders and their business culture

- to identify the level of support and resistance that exists for the project

---

3   The Project Manager must identify how the current culture will change when the transformation solution is implemented. This early assessment will be used to adjust rewards and reinforcements for long-term sustainment of the change, addressed in Step 10: Sustain the Transformation—Create the New Norm.

A Stakeholder Readiness analysis provides the Project Manager and Project Team with a baseline to formulate a plan for developing targeted activities to build the critical mass of support that creates a tipping point. See further discussion in Chapter 7 (Create a Multi-Pronged Approach in Preparing for Transformation).

Create a Stakeholder Map

To prepare for the collection of information for the Stakeholder Readiness analysis, begin by making a shareholder map that includes:

- a comprehensive listing, by name and title/role, of all employees who are affected by the change

- a reporting structure

- a description of how each role is affected (with templates to indicate key categories such as 'training required' and 'new behaviour or skill' and each category having a related rating scale, from high to low)

NOTE: Keep a separate executive stakeholder map. It should assess both support and readiness for the transformation for each executive affected by, or who can affect, the change. The Project Manager and Sponsor should continually review this map as a reference for developing strategies to maintain and increase support.

Interview Key Internal Stakeholders

Determine the baseline level of support among key stakeholders by asking the following questions:

- Do they accept and support the reasons and need for transformation?

- Do they understand the major elements of the transformation project and what will change?

- Do they believe that the transformation project solution is the right solution? Will it solve the organizational problem and move the organization forward? Will it help them meet their function's key objectives? What part do they like? Not like? Why?

- Are they concerned about the project work and their resource time and effort required to prepare for and implement the change?

- What are their concerns about the change? Organizationally? Functionally? Personally?

- Are their concerns based on:

  ◊ technology changes or issues?

  ◊ process changes or issues?

  ◊ people impact?

- What suggestions do they have for the project and solution to work better?

If there are too many key stakeholders to interview individually, organize focus group sessions. Cover off similar questions.

Interview Key External Stakeholders
In identifying all stakeholders that the transformation will impact in some way, the Project Manager and Project Sponsor

must also consider external stakeholders. Interviews/sessions are required with them if the following is true:

For Customers The transformation will change the services or products offered or the way those services or products are received (e.g., a merger may require rebranding or a different mix of products/services). Contact must be carefully engineered, working with key internal managers or specialists who are accountable for managing customer contact and customer relations. Timing and messaging are important, since you will want to give enough notice to prepare for changes but also want to wait until you are sure of the solution and launch date for those changes before communicating.

For Suppliers The transformation will change the way the supply process will work (e.g., ERP systems will typically create changes in order numbering systems and could have significant impact on suppliers). The Project Manager should work with the internal stakeholder who is accountable for managing the supplier relationship. Often, suppliers require a lot of lead time in order to be prepared for changes they must make when the transformation solution is implemented. For instance, new systems sometimes require new product numbering. As a result, for a smooth transition, suppliers may need ramp-up time to make their changes.

Stakeholder Readiness work provides a baseline picture of where and what support and resistance there is for your transformation project and solution. It gives the Project Team all the raw data they need to work on developing a change readiness plan to achieve a critical mass of support for the project transformation. This activity must be done early enough to allow time to create and implement a plan for developing more support and reducing major resistance.

STOP POINT

The results of the Stakeholder Readiness work may require the Project Team and Project Sponsor to modify plans. A hard look needs to be taken at the project to judge whether disagreements with the solution or suggestions to modify it are based on real flaws, solvable issues or concerns, or simply resistance to change. The Project Sponsor may need to have difficult conversations with Steering Committee members if key senior or influential stakeholders are identified as major roadblocks to implementing the transformation. These discussions may have to take place with the crossover manager (often the CEO) to determine the right course of action. The transformation project cannot proceed until it has been verified that there is still senior management/key stakeholder commitment to the transformation solution.

CHAPTER 7

Step 7: Create a Multi-Pronged Approach in Preparing for Transformation

Never doubt that a small group of thoughtful, committed citizens can change the world. Indeed, it is the only thing that ever has.
—Margaret Mead

My Step 7 Story: Why Don't You Just Say I'm Sorry?

During the mid-1980s I held the role of internal Organizational Effectiveness Manager for a division of a major multinational chemical organization. The organization was introducing a Japanese-style teamwork approach called Quality Circles. The theory was that organizations could achieve greater productivity from front-line workers if they were given training to problem-solve production problems and the autonomy to solve problems themselves.

This was one of the first jobs I had after graduating with my MBA. During my studies, I was a research assistant for Dr. Olga Crocker, a well-known professor[1] who was in the process of writing one of the better-known Canadian books on the subject of Quality Circles. I was full of positive energy, believing I was an expert on the topic of Quality Circles and could help the organization implement this work-culture change effectively. In classic consulting style, I began interviewing and collecting data from all stakeholders, devised a training course that I delivered to both supervisors and front-line production workers on problem-solving techniques, and launched the program.

Although the interest appeared to be strong during learning sessions, after the launch of the program we had a major problem. Quality Circle participation was voluntary, and I expected a very high sign-up rate (70% to 80%) of employees wanting to join the teams. After three or four weeks, fewer than 10% of the employees had joined the program. I was baffled and very disappointed. Why wouldn't employees want to join a program that would make their working lives so much more interesting and give them more control over the changes that occurred in their workplace?

I began talking to senior managers and supervisors to gain some insight into where we went wrong. They had none. A few weeks later, I was out walking the shop floor when the union shop steward pulled me aside. He said that he knew I was disappointed and asked me if I wanted to know the reason

---

1   Olga Crocker, *Quality Circles: A Guide to Participation and Productivity* (New York: Facts on File, 1985).

for this lack of interest. Of course I was interested, and we arranged to talk over a coffee. He told me that the reason was simple: union staff were still very upset that management had not been up front with them in a past employee program that resulted in some unfair work practices and preferential treatment of certain employees. Everyone knew that the program was a failure, but management never admitted their mistakes. This happened just before I joined the company. People still mistrusted management, and they were naturally suspicious of joining another management productivity 'scheme' that would somehow affect them adversely. I asked him what he believed would help develop trust and leave them open to joining this new program. He replied that it would be good if the company President stood in front of everyone and said "I'm sorry" for what happened before.

I took this information back to the Executive Team in my next report. When asked by the company President what I thought we should do, I suggested we hold a company-wide communication session where he would stand before everyone and explain what happened in the last effort and then give employees his personal commitment that things would be different this time. He agreed and went a step better on the actual day.

The President stood up in front of the full production crew and started the session by saying: "I am here to talk about our Quality Circle program, but before I go any further, I want to say to each and every one of you that I am sorry for the mistakes we made in implementing our last program." The President took the union shop steward's suggestions, virtually using his words, and offered no excuses for the errors. He went on to say that he and the management team have tried to learn from these mistakes and believed that they had it right this time. Furthermore, they were going to keep open feedback channels and means through which any employee could express dissatisfaction—either anonymously or by name—and management would respond to all concerns.

A week after that presentation, 50% of the staff had joined a Quality Circle. Two weeks after that, 75% of the staff had joined.

Step 7 Activities

Once the Project Manager has completed the initial Stakeholder Readiness baseline assessment, a plan to build a critical mass of support must be developed and managed throughout the rest of the life of the transformation project. Although Steps 7 and 8 are separate, their activities are really quite fluid. The Project Manager will create a plan while concurrently engaging with key stakeholders. The goal is to look for opportunities to increase support and commitment for the transformation project and solution by:

- assuring stakeholders who are fearful of learning new skills that training, coaching, and support will be provided before, during, and after launch of the change

- listening to and understanding real concerns, and working together with stakeholders to try to eliminate them

Identify and Prioritize the Most Critical Stakeholders

As in the preceding Steps, executive stakeholders are the initial focus. The Project Manager and the Project Sponsor must develop a plan to continually develop and maintain executive support throughout the preparation and implementation of the transformation, but the plan should identify and prioritize all stakeholder groups.

The best way to think of successfully implementing change in an organization is to work on developing commitment and support in the following order:

1. The Project Sponsor and Project Team

   The Project Sponsor should be the head cheerleader for the project transformation, relentlessly working to keep it a strategic priority with the executive group.

2. Key executives and the Executive Steering Committee

   The executive and its Steering Committee must truly believe that the transformation project is a top strategic priority and that the project solution is the best solution. Each Committee member must put skin in the game by providing resources and budget and by supporting the project until the transformation is complete.

3. Other key internal stakeholders or stakeholder groups most affected by the change or most affecting its successful outcome

   This group could include:

   - senior operational managers who have large numbers of stakeholders reporting to them who are the most affected by the change

   - Specialists who own and/or manage existing legacy systems or processes that are being replaced or modified by the change

   Oftentimes, these key specialist stakeholders start out being skeptical, or even resistant or negative, to the transformation solution. A common reason for this is that, frequently, they are the ones who created and championed the legacy system or process that is being replaced. Years ago, one colleague told me it is like "calling their baby ugly." The Project Manager should seek out these individuals early and enlist their help and advice by saying something like this: "You have been one of the company's most valuable employees in managing this system/process until now. It was the right decision for the time, but circumstances have changed and that requires us to change again. We would love to have you on board to help us understand and learn from how you initially got people on board and how you made the current system/process work for us for so long and to get your insights on how we can make this solution work."

The other thing the Project Manager should do for these 'past system/process heroes' is give them recognition for their achievements. These accolades should be real and deserved, but organizations often forget about a small group of engineering wizards and hard, dedicated workers who have been holding together systems and processes with 'bits of string.' You will be amazed at how quickly you can turn a potential project resister into a staunch, loyal, and valuable project supporter by using this tactic.

4. A 'critical mass' of stakeholders who will help create a tipping point

The Project Manager must judge who and where the key stakeholders are that will most quickly create a tipping point of support and commitment for the transformation solution. The following tactics will help Project Managers focus their efforts on the right group of stakeholders:

- Find the greatest number of stakeholders affected by the change who have the most to gain by the project. DO NOT begin with the group that will be the most challenging and resistant, that has the least to gain, or that may even suffer negative consequences from the change.

- Find an influential project advocate and involve them in strategizing and communicating. This could be anyone from a Steering Committee member to a technical specialist who is well known and well thought of within the organization. Seek out their advice, and discuss ways you could involve them in helping develop support and commitment throughout the project.

5. External stakeholders

If there are vendors or customers whose interactions with or services provided to the organization will change due to the transformation, they should be contacted early. For vendors, ensure that they understand what the changes are and provide enough lead time for them to successfully adapt to the change. For customers, judge whether there is an opportunity to present the results of the transformation as a benefit to service or a value they will receive.

With priorities laid out, the Project Manager should lead the key activities to find and act upon these opportunities.

Develop an Executive Stakeholder Change Readiness Plan

An executive Stakeholder Readiness plan needs to be developed separately. Key executives who are impacted or can impact the transformation project must be given individual attention and their support and commitment level individually tracked. This is not because they should be given preferential or deferential treatment due to their elevated position in the organization. It is because their support and commitment can most quickly and significantly affect your project. One disgruntled senior executive can often place barriers in your way that make successful project completion impossible or that derail user adoption.

SCHEDULE REGULAR MEETINGS

The Project Manager should first develop a regular meeting schedule with individual executive stakeholders (priority group 2 above) to review their support and readiness levels. There are tools and templates to effectively assess the level of executive support. The Project Manager should work with the Project Sponsor to develop this schedule and a strategy to keep commitment high among key executives. The Project Sponsor is accountable for delivering this plan, probably in tandem with the Project Manager.

Executive meeting frequency will depend upon the importance of support from the particular executive for the success of the transformation and the executive's level of support and readiness as indicated in early discussions: the higher the criticality and the lower the support, the more frequent the contact required.

Meeting focus should be, first, on working to eliminate barriers and objections to the executive's full support and, next, on assuring him or her that the organization and the executive's group will be supported by the Project Team to ensure their function is ready to adapt to the change. The emphasis should be on highlighting the advantages that the transformation solution brings to each executive in helping them meet their functional and personal business goals. Keep in mind that most resistance among senior executives occurs when the Project Team has failed to show them how the transformation will help them be more successful in achieving their business function and personal objectives or failed to give them confidence and comfort in describing how their area will be supported through the difficult change transition period.

LOOK FOR PROJECT ADVOCATES

Every Project Team needs help in selling and developing support for a major organizational change. One very good tactic that the Project Sponsor and Project Manager can use is to identify and collaborate with project advocates. A project advocate is an executive ally who has either a strategic reason and/or a personal belief for actively supporting the project and transformation. The Project Sponsor should use this individual, or individuals, to help continually develop and maintain support with other executives and to help obtain key votes in the Steering Committee (priority group 2 above). More frequent meetings should be set up with project advocates to strategize on eliminating issues and barriers and developing more support.

Develop a Change Readiness Plan for Key Internal Stakeholders

In looking at the rest of the organization, the Project Manager's first attention should go to key stakeholders or stakeholder groups that are most affected by the change (priority group

3 above). The data collected in Step 6 (Assess the Degree of Support and Resistance for the Transformation) will help categorize and prioritize stakeholders.

Within this group, 'low-hanging fruit'—those who are most impacted by the transformation change and most likely to benefit—are the most likely to be receptive to the change. They are the ones whom the Project Manager wants to identify and plan for first. The internal Stakeholder Readiness plan should address the impact on them in terms of process, technology, and people changes.

PROCESS CHANGE

Many organizations do not take the time needed to determine what process changes are required to making a transformation, particularly in technology, successful. If the Team was resourced effectively, there will be Functional Leads assigned with the accountability of ensuring that the transformation works for major business work processes. One of the major deliverables of these Functional Leads is to conduct process review sessions in business areas that will be most affected by the transformation. The purpose of these sessions is to identify and address changes in roles and workflow.

PROCESS REVIEW METHODOLOGY STEPS

1. Identify which major business processes will be affected by the transformation.

2. Conduct Process Role Mapping sessions.

   • Involve subject-matter experts who currently have roles in the process.

- Have the solution expert facilitate the session(s). This would be either the Functional Lead or someone on the Functional Team who understands how the process works, new roles, and workflow in the new transformation state.

- Ensure the facilitator focuses on identifying changes in the Future State, *not improving the Current State.* The goal of the exercise is to identify what it will take to get to the Future State successfully. If opportunities arise to improve areas out of scope for the transformation, 'park' them for the functional areas accountable for that process to work on it in their own priority timetable. There is no value in spending time to identify the Current State. The facilitator will present the Future State process to internal subject-matter experts, who will validate what is new, modified, or the same in the process.

- Identify the process in a Process Role Map. There are many ways to do this, but the most common is to create 'swim lane' charts that list major process steps down the left-hand side, organizational roles across the top, and a process flow chart showing sub-steps of work done.

3. Highlight areas on the completed Process Role Map where:

   - current work will stop

   - new work will begin

   - current work will be modified

4. For each of the highlighted areas, describe what people, process, and/or technology will change and require preparation.

5. Prioritize and assign a schedule for doing the transformation work. It may require setting up a Working Sub-Group to get this preparatory work done; progress should be reported to the Project Team.

6. Work with managers accountable for managing that business process to create a Process Readiness plan. Functional Leads will take the results of their process review sessions to the operational managers who are accountable for managing the process and help them prioritize work to get their areas ready for process changes required for the transformation solution to be successful. Criteria presented for this prioritization will include:

   - the importance of the process step for making the change successful

   - the timing (Does the new or modified process step need to be complete before launching the solution? Within three months? Later?)

   - the complexity and resources/budget required to accomplish the change

   - the lead time required to get the work done

   - the new roles or different volume of roles required to get the job done

   - the new skills/training required for existing roles

   - the communication required for changes in roles

The Functional Lead will offer advice, training, coaching, and communication support to the operational manager accountable for making these changes to his or her area.

NOTE: The Training and Communication Leads should be involved in this process. At a minimum, they should examine the results of the process review sessions. They should sit in on key process review sessions to ensure that they understand the Future State Process and the impact on training and communication.

TECHNOLOGY CHANGE

When your large transformation is driven by or includes a large technology component, the solution needs to be assessed by your internal IT professionals to ensure that it aligns with the overall business architecture, technical architecture, and general IT vision for the organization. It means that the most effective tools and systems are being used, that they are integrated with other systems being used, and that the organization will be ready to implement and maintain those systems and technology.

NON-TRANSFORMATION WORK

Although the 10-Step change methodology does not cover the technical aspect of the change in depth, it is worth mentioning a few key points that result in major problems in many technology transformation projects. Some technology changes will be identified in process review sessions for all strategic transformation projects. However, in technology transformation projects, there are technology change issues that are unique. Project Managers must be prepared to address two areas that continually cause major increases in scope, time, and budget in technology transformations.

1. Problems in the development of interfaces

    Most major systems implementations—whether they are ERP systems, Business Intelligence, Enterprise Project Portfolio systems, or others—require a significant amount of work to be designed on interfaces that link those systems to other key systems in the organization. These linkages are usually complicated, often requiring creative thinking about how to make the connection between systems that have little in common and were not designed to be linked. Many times, good solutions are not achieved in time, and manual processes are introduced until better solutions are created. Interface challenges can create huge project delays and even derail a technology transformation.

2. Quality of legacy data: avoid GIGO (garbage in/garbage out)

    The other most common problem in technology transformation projects is the underestimation or lack of awareness of legacy data issues. Typically, one of the big benefits communicated in major systems implementation is that the new system will allow data and reporting to be timely and more accurately produced. However, if existing data is inaccurate, the new system won't fix it. Ironically, it may actually make things worse until the problem is fixed. Data must first be cleansed, and then proper data management and data governance practices must be put in place so that good data will continue to be collected. Often, the job of cleansing data and cleaning up data-collecting processes is so monumental in time and complexity that it blows the project scope and schedule right out of the water. Therefore, it is important for the Project Manager and the Project Sponsor to get a clear picture very early in the project of what the risks are in addressing data. It is important to have the organization's most senior data management guru involved in the early part of this process and, at minimum, kept as a key subject-matter expert throughout the development of the technology transformation solution ... at least until all data-related work is complete.

PEOPLE CHANGE

The last area of impact is how the change will affect all stakeholders.

Most of the people change will be identified in the Process and Technology Readiness work; collect all of that data under the 'people change' category. In addition, develop a Stakeholder Readiness questionnaire to gather information directly from stakeholders on areas of change.

Prioritize the Impacts

If there will be any major impact on people resulting from technology or process change, or being driven by the need for restructuring, merging, or downsizing, here is the priority in which these impacts should be addressed.

#1 Job loss   This is obviously the largest impact. It requires early planning; Human Resources and union involvement (if applicable); and a plan for notifying and communicating with potentially affected individuals, their peers, and the organization. There is a big difference in how the transformation will be run and communicated if there is job loss. It will also add tasks to the Critical Path of the project, such as notification periods to affected employees.

#2 Relocation   This can be as traumatic and impactful as job loss. At a minimum, it is disruptive to employees' existing commuting routine. At a maximum, it could be equivalent to job loss. If relocation is far enough away to be impractical for families to move, it must be treated the same as job loss.

These first two people impacts must be considered very early in the planning process for the following reasons:

- If unionized employees are affected, there often need to be lengthy notification periods.

- Human Resources may need time to notify those affected, develop options, prepare packages, and properly communicate with them.

- Human Resources may need time to reclassify and post new or modified positions, a process that may take weeks or months, depending upon whether the positions can be placed internally or externally, and what market conditions are like at the time.

The next two priority impacts are related to roles that will significantly change due to the transformation.

#3 Significant job redesign   First, the Project Manager, or relevant Project Team Leads (perhaps Functional Leads), should review changes to roles with the manager accountable for managing those roles, to assess whether these changes will alter the category or level of job for that role. If there are significant role changes, Human Resources should be involved in these discussions. Human Resources typically has industry or corporate standards for the reclassification of roles. If reclassification is required, expect your Critical Path to be extended since there may be a need to post and even hire for newly created positions. At a minimum, there will be significant retraining for incumbents.

#4 Training Training or retraining will likely need to take place for incumbents to learn new skills for new roles. Through process review sessions, it is often discovered that certain organizational roles will need to change substantively when the transformation is implemented. For instance, a new system may require an analytical role to now be more administrative in nature (if the system performs that analysis), or a role that was administrative in nature may now require analytical skills as a new system provides new opportunities for additional or deeper analysis. In other cases, there may simply be new or modified process steps that require new skills that a particular role did not require before. The Project Training Lead should manage the training or retraining process to ensure that all new process training is built into customized training for the appropriate stakeholders and prerequisite knowledge is identified.

Develop a Change Readiness Plan for Critical Mass Stakeholders—The Value of Change Agents

The next task is to develop a prioritized plan to address issues and concerns from stakeholder groups identified as the prime target in gaining a critical mass of support (priority group 4 above). Categorize issues in these high priority groups, and set up meetings or focus groups to gain more insights about their concerns or issues.

The Project Sponsor, Project Manager, and other key team members have all been acting as 'change agents' to try to garner support for the transformation. At this point the Project Manager needs to identify and recruit other change agents throughout the organization to help market and influence the changes planned in the transformation. There are many definitions of a change agent, the simplest perhaps being "a person who possesses enough knowledge and power to guide and facilitate the change effort."[2]

However, none of the definitions that I have found captures the true essence of the role of a change agent, especially when significant change is being introduced into the organization. To provide more insight on what a good change agent should look like for a major organizational transformation, here is a more comprehensive list of traits:

- Displays knowledge about both the transformation solution and how it will benefit and affect the organization's strategic direction and operations

- Truly believes in, is passionate about, and is an active cheerleader in the adoption of the transformation solution and the Project Plan to achieve that solution — and this deep passion and belief inspires others to believe in it as well

- Is driven and tenacious in implementing the Plan and in overcoming hurdles to achieve the ultimate goal

- Is a superior communicator, particularly in listening skills, with a perpetual focus on uncovering issues and barriers to achieving the ultimate transformation goal

---

2   Steven McShane, *Organizational Behaviour*, 3rd ed. (Toronto: McGraw-Hill Ryerson Limited, 1998), 404.

CREATE AND FACILITATE A CHANGE CHAMPION COMMITTEE

The Project Manager, Project Sponsor, and Project Team need help to develop a critical mass of support and commitment for the transformation project in time for the Project Launch. One effective way to develop support and commitment more broadly and quickly throughout the organization is to create and launch a Change Champion Committee (also often called a Change Network).

A Change Champion Committee is a core group of senior change agents who meet as a group and work individually to share information, provide input, disseminate information, and help implement change-related activities throughout and within an organization to assist in a large organizational transformation. During the preparation before your transformation launch, this group will help make your plan relevant and meaningful to affected staff. If you have done a good job in selecting and involving this group, it will be key in driving and sustaining the change after launch.

Change Champion Committee Membership

Once the support and commitment for the transformation solution has been received from the Executive Steering Committee, the Project Sponsor should present the purpose and need for creating a Change Champion Committee for the project. The Change Champions will represent each major function affected by the change; be appointed by the Steering Committee; and, as a group, be chaired by the Project Manager and/or Project Sponsor. The ideal Change Champion candidate:

- is a senior operational individual (typically one level below the Steering Committee)

- knows the end-to-end business operations of that function very well

- is known and respected by other employees in that function

- is a good communicator

- is assertive

- has a positive view of the transformation solution

The Communication Lead and Project Team Coordinator may also be standing members of this committee. It is useful to have the Communication Lead attend these meetings both to present communications early to this group and to hear how project communication is being received. The Change Champion Committee can work directly with the Communication Lead to help shape or reshape messages for better understanding by their groups. The Project Team Coordinator could attend to help administer action items and other coordination needs.

Change Champions should both be assigned and volunteer. It is unproductive and potentially disruptive to have a resentful committee member on the Team, or one who is resistant to the transformation solution. Clarify what the accountabilities and time commitments will be before individuals sign up for the role.

Managing the Change Champion Committee

The goal is to make the Change Champion Committee autonomous since these senior operational managers are the true change agents of the transformation. The following are typical elements in managing this group:

- Initially, the Committee should be managed by the Project Manager and/or Project Sponsor.

- The Project Manager should set the agenda, facilitate discussion, and coach or provide learning on the solution when required.

- Meetings should be held monthly and on an ad hoc basis in between if required.

- At Committee start-up, Change Champions will need a thorough presentation of the transformation solution and the Project Plan.

- The focus is on dealing with issues, concerns, and a discussion of strategy for how to increase support, commitment, and the ultimate adoption of the transformation solution.

- Milestone decisions and major project communication should be presented to the Change Champions before being disseminated throughout the organization so they can help customize messages.

- Leadership should eventually be shifted to a non-Project Team member.

- The Change Champion Committee should be formed soon after true executive support has been achieved and after the solid Project Charter and Project Plan have been completed.

- The Committee should continue to meet for about three to six months after the launch of the transformation solution so members can help assess initial adoption and provide input for necessary adjustments and communication. It should be the group members' decision how long the Committee will operate. They may decide to disband several weeks after the transformation solution is implemented or may want to continue meeting to assess longer-term adoption and sustenance. The group may also evolve into a Community of Practice.

- The Project Manager will continue to attend Committee meetings for, at most, a few months past the launch of the transformation solution, progressively moving into more of an advisory role.

Develop a Change Readiness Plan for External Stakeholders

In Step 6, the Project Manager determined whether there was a need to include external stakeholders in the transformation project plan, depending on whether they were impacted. If this impact is validated in Step 6, a change readiness plan is needed for customers and suppliers.

FOR CUSTOMERS

An initial presentation of the transformation solution to customers should:

- highlight the transformation 'story,' outlining the rationale and vision for the change

- focus on the changes and benefits to customers

- present timing for the changes

- describe the preparation required for the change (ideally very little or seamless to customers, unless changes are to improve their product, the supply chain, or cost of product or service)

- present a communication schedule (including progress updates, solution demonstrations, and launch dates)

- conduct a transformation solution demonstration. Customers need to see what the change will look like for them. Ideally, this should be done two to four weeks before changes occur, when key customers can be given a demonstration of exactly what the change will look like for them. Focus only on what will be relevant and beneficial to customers. Simulations or real-life demonstrations are ideal in showing customers how their operations will be improved on the launch date and will also, at the right time, heighten awareness of the change about to occur

---

STOP POINT

Unless the transformation will change products or services dramatically, it is unlikely that customers will raise objections to it. If the transformation does dramatically change products and/or services to customers, be prepared to listen to and appropriately react to objections to the change. Customers will obviously need to believe changes will provide real benefits. If the Project Team and internal Customer Relationship Leads cannot convince them of these benefits, the project transformation is officially on hold until this situation is resolved.

IMPORTANT NOTE: It is more likely that the transformation solution will either provide real benefits that will be easy to sell to customers or cause only minor changes to products and/

or services they receive. For customers: don't make a mountain out of a molehill with your transformation project. It can create more confusion, or even dissatisfaction, if the organization communicates to customers about an upcoming organizational change that will have little impact on them. Only communicate aspects of the change that will affect them or that your marketing team believes customers will care about. Unless the objective is to expand services and product offerings, most transformation projects have little impact on customers. Sometimes the best result is for customers not to notice a change at all. Be careful what you present, to whom, and when.

FOR SUPPLIERS

Like customers, suppliers should only be briefed on the transformation solution as it pertains to and impacts them. The initial presentation to them should be similar to that for customers, with these differences:

- Highlight the transformation 'story,' outlining the rationale and vision for the change, but focus on the supplier impact.

- Focus on the changes required by suppliers. These should also be presented as long-term benefits, although it might require initial work from suppliers to prepare for supply process changes. Successful organizations treat their suppliers as true partners, creating win-win situations. Organizations should treat suppliers very similarly to customers.

- Think of the whole supply chain process and how it will impact suppliers.

- Include a working group discussion period where the Project Manager, or other Project Lead, will lead a discussion with suppliers to both ensure they understand changes and provide the opportunity to identify other changes. This will likely be only the first of more working group sessions required in order for the Project Team and suppliers to work together on a seamless plan for change.

- Present timing for changes and the timing window to prepare for changes.

- Present a communication schedule (including progress updates, solution demonstrations, and launch dates).

- Conduct transformation project supplier working group sessions to review the supply chain process to ensure all preparations are made in time for the changes to be launched.

In the end, suppliers will not dictate terms for the transformation solution, but it is critical for the Project Manager to establish a partnership arrangement to make as easy a transition as possible for suppliers.

FOR OTHER EXTERNAL STAKEHOLDERS

Through discussions with internal and external stakeholders, the Project Manager may uncover the need to consider change readiness plans for other external stakeholders if they can affect, or will be affected by, the transformation solution. Examples of such external groups are government agencies, associations, and regulatory bodies.

With technology-driven or process-driven changes, the change effects on external stakeholders other than customers or suppliers are minimal. Typically, these changes relate to formatting of information, or methods of transmitting or receiving information. Also, the acceptance and support of changes by these other external stakeholders are typically not as critical as the acceptance and support of changes by internal stakeholders, customers, or suppliers.

CHAPTER 8

Step 8: Manage the Transformation – Reset the Project Plan at Milestones or Gates

Do not repeat the tactics which have gained you one victory, but let your methods be regulated by the infinite variety of circumstances.
—Sun Tzu

My Step 8 Story: Everything Changes ... Even the Project Plan

The largest transformation project I ever managed as a Program Manager Lead was a government project that significantly transformed the business model, the business processes, and the whole organizational structure and roles of six thousand employees. The project lasted three years. I collaborated with the Project Sponsor, an Assistant Deputy Minister, to develop an integrated Project Plan that was to be used as a repeatable and scalable approach to the redesign of the business processes and organizational structure of each division of the ministry.

Over the course of the three years it took to implement the changes across the ministry, I conducted six Team sessions that I called Project Integration Sessions. Each of these lasted at least half a day (three of them, a full day). The first session was conducted as we launched the Project Team work. After each major division implementation, we conducted another Project Integration Session, applying learning and changes obtained to date. After every Project Integration Session, we changed our project integration model. In at least three instances, that resulted in us changing the scope or schedule for implementing the next phase of work.

By the third or fourth Project Integration Session, Team Leads were quite tired of going through the exercise, but all commented on the usefulness and necessity of the exercise to continually reset the Project Plan.

Conducting six Project Integration Sessions over the course of a transformation project—even a three-year project—may seem excessive. However, given the results of each session, I would do exactly the same thing if I were managing the project again.

Step 8 Activities

This step may seem to be more of a project management step than a transformation project-specific step. However, although it mostly covers just good project management practice, it is so critical to the success of your transformation project that it has been included as a separate step.

Transformation projects frequently falter as soon as changes in scope, time, and/or budget are presented.[1] When these changes arise, executives and other senior stakeholders will often perceive the project as either poorly planned or poorly executed. Stakeholders who are resistant to the transformation will use this information as ammunition, aiming to garner support for their resistance among other employees who are 'on the fence' with their support. Changes to the Project Plan must be expected, planned for, and communicated if support is to be maintained and to grow throughout the planning and implementation of the transformation. This may not be a great concern for a project that is only a few months long, but the longer the project, the greater the concern.

Experienced Project Managers know that a Project Plan (and even a Project Charter) is a living, changing thing. Accurate detailed plans can really only be created for up to three months (or less) with longer-term milestones or gates. The Project Plan is iterative because there is always a discovery process during the design of the solution that uncovers new risks, issues, costs, and opportunities. For transformation projects, the following practices are important for successfully managing longer-term projects (anything more than six months).

---

1   Any changes that result in the project achieving the goals in less time or under budget with the same or increased scope will not require 'selling' the change to stakeholders.

Communicate the Iterative Nature of the Project Plan

Most senior executives whom I have worked with don't understand project management. When you bring a Project Charter and then a High-Level Project Plan to the executive group, they expect that the scope and schedule are carved in stone and that those are your performance targets. Although that is the intention, all experienced Project Managers know that the Plan is an iterative process because the work done uncovers unknown information and results that can change it. It is also why contingency time and costs must be built into the Plan, to be used if and when required. This does not mean that the project shouldn't have performance target goals but that these goals will almost surely need to be changed and managed throughout the life of the project.

It is the job of the Project Manager and Project Sponsor to make sure executives understand the iterative nature of a long-term Project Plan and how the project is being managed and then to manage the executives' expectations.

PROJECT MANAGER'S RESPONSIBILITY

More specifically, the Project Manager must:

- educate the Steering Committee, Project Team, and other key stakeholders as required about how the iterative nature of long-term projects often changes scope, budget, and/or schedule—give examples

- identify, to the Steering Committee only, early unknowns and risks that may affect scope, time, and/or budget

- state that scope, timing, and/or budget elements of the projects could change:

- ◊ at any time when analysis uncovers an additional issue or piece of work previously unknown (e.g., data challenges in legacy systems not analyzed before)

- ◊ at the end of a milestone period or at project gates, as the next phase of work is detailed

- ◊ after planned Project Integration Sessions

PROJECT SPONSOR'S RESPONSIBILITY

Further to the Project Manager's explanation of how and why scope, timing, and/or budget elements could potentially change, the Project Sponsor should state that should that occur, options will be presented to the Steering Committee for a decision. Often three options will be given, with a recommendation from the Project Team.

Option 1: Status quo   Present the risks and likely outcomes if no changes to scope, timing, and/or budget are made.

Option 2: Decrease of scope   Present a smaller scope for the project that would still accomplish much of what is required but will stay within the original budget and timing proposed. This option often includes a phased-in solution approach.

Option 3: Increase of budget/time   Propose an increase in timing and/or budget based on uncovering of additional pieces of work that must be completed for the project to meet its stated objectives. An increase in timing is an option usually taken when the additional scope identified is more important than staying on time or budget. An increase in budget only is usually an option when the timing of the solution is immovable for a critical business reason.

Other options—variations of options 2 and 3—may be presented, but it is recommended to not have too many for Committee consideration.

Manage a Rolling Six-Week to Three-Month Project Plan

The Plan could be updated monthly or more frequently. The Project Manager must balance the benefit of managing a real-time accurate plan with the cost of administering this effort. This work effort would ideally be managed by a Project Coordinator. The value of managing a rolling Project Plan is that it forces the Project Team to continually assess any slippage, issues, challenges, or changes that would affect the overall project (whether in quality, scheduling, or scope). It will save time and money to catch changes early.

Conduct Milestone-Linked Project Integration Sessions

The Project Manager should be constantly assessing the Plan and making adjustments as required. However, it is sometimes hard to see large changes coming when everyone on the Project Team is going at full throttle to complete deliverables. As presented in my story at the beginning of this chapter, it is invaluable and essential for the Project Manager to conduct Project Integration Sessions at key milestone times in the project. These will help the Project Team not only identify potential schedule or scope changes ahead of them but may also give the Team time to develop mitigating strategies to help avoid these changes. Here are some recommendations on how to prepare and conduct a Project Integration Session.

IDENTIFY SUITABLE MILESTONES

Examples of milestones, or gates, that are good times to conduct a Project Integration Session and reassess your Project Plan include:

- after a key analysis is conducted that uncovers major project information previously unknown (e.g., you completed a data analysis on legacy systems requiring interface development, a stakeholder analysis, or a major process analysis)

- after a major phase of work is done, and a new phase is to be detailed on the Plan (e.g., you just finished business requirements on a new business process and uncovered a new need for a total overhaul/re-engineering of a major business process)

- if a number of new major risks are identified, and it's likely the Project Plan needs to be reset (e.g., you uncovered a major skills and/or capacity gap in an area of the business that is key to the success of the transformation— this might cause months of reskilling/training and/or recruitment to shore up this gap)

PREPARE FOR THE PROJECT INTEGRATION SESSION

The Project Manager will need to spend some time preparing for the session to get good results.

- Invite all Project Leads, and anyone else accountable for developing and delivering major sections of the Plan (every part of the Plan should be represented by someone accountable for it).

- Make attendance mandatory.

- Schedule the session for a full day. This will be a working session, and you need to schedule the time required to get it right. Make it clear to participants that "we will stay until we have completed the work." In some cases, it may require going into the evening ... or continuing the next day.

- Task each Team Lead to prepare and present each element of their work plan (at work package/high level), highlighting changes or new elements of:

  ◊ what is to be delivered

  ◊ when it is to be delivered

  ◊ resources required

  ◊ interdependencies (both what she/he is dependent on receiving from other streams of work and what other streams of work are dependent upon in receiving from her/his stream of work)

  ◊ issues creating barriers on getting work done on time, on budget, or at the quality level required

  ◊ risks for the future

- Set strict time maximums for Team Lead presentations (total time should work out to half of the day at most, giving time for project integration discussion).

- Organize room preparations, 'brown paper' exercise, etc.

CONDUCT THE PROJECT INTEGRATION SESSION

There is more than one way to conduct this type of session, and below is a format that has worked well for me. But first, three general recommendations:

- Tightly manage the time allowed for each lead to present their piece, since all must be completed in the morning.

- Conduct the workshop as a large 'brown paper' exercise (or equivalent electronic version), where each element presented will be posted on the wall (sticky notes work well, with different colours for project work streams, work activities, interdependencies, and resources). It is essential that all participants continually see the whole picture on the wall (or screen) as the Plan is being reviewed.

- Focus on what has changed, instead of reviewing all deliverables.

Day's Agenda
MORNING PRESENTATIONS

1. The Project Sponsor kicks off the event and emphasizes the criticality of the activity.

2. The Project Manager facilitates the event, beginning with the usual introductions and appropriate review of agenda and process.

3. Individual Team Leads make their presentations.

4. Any discussion should be focused only on clarification of each presentation rather than on developing solutions or debating issues or risks. Take the time you need to develop understanding of the full picture and new issues and risks.

AFTERNOON DISCUSSION

5. With the Project Manager as facilitator, review each element of the Plan at a high level in logical Critical Path

order. End with a review of support activity areas (e.g., Communication, Human Resources).

6. Have each Lead once again highlight changes or new elements of the Plan.

7. Ask the group:

    • What recent work has uncovered changes or potential changes to the Plan?

    • What do new interdependencies do to other streams' plans? Have other stream Leads add work and resources to their Plan (on brown paper) for all to see and highlight.

    • What are solution options for issues? If not readily solvable by the Team, assign a logical owner to devise a solution.

    • What is the probability of new risks? What work needs to be done to address risks? Review the same as issues above.

8. Brainstorm potential mitigation actions to address new issues or risks that will still allow the Plan to be completed on schedule, on budget, and within scope.

9. Capture Team decisions: with each change that is agreed upon after discussion, and taking into account mitigation actions to minimize the effect of these changes, adjust the Critical Path and/or resources if required.

FOLLOW UP ON THE PROJECT INTEGRATION SESSION
After the session is completed, the Project Manager is accountable for taking the data from the day and creating a reset

Project Plan according to all input, with mitigation actions as required. The next Project Management Team session should be dedicated to presenting the reset Plan, highlighting changes to Critical Path, interdependencies, key issues, and risks.

Typically, the Project Manager will need a two-hour session, perhaps extending the next project management meeting (usually only an hour). The Project Manager should expect additional behind-the-scenes work to get all elements of the changes into the Plan.

It is important that, at the end of the review of the reset Plan, the Project Manager obtains a personal commitment from each stream Lead that they will be accountable for this reset Plan. This may occur during the session or individually after the session. The team will need to present a united front to the Project Sponsor and executives when presenting changes to the scope or schedule of the Plan.

Communicate the Results of the Project Integration Session

At minimum, if no substantive changes were uncovered at the Project Integration Session, the Project Sponsor and Project Manager must confirm and communicate the next phase of work to the Steering Committee and other key stakeholders.

If the Project Integration Session uncovered a need to consider changing the project's scope, budget, or timing, the Project Sponsor and Project Manager should create a few options and a recommendation for the Steering Committee to consider for decision-making (see the "Project Manager's Responsibility" and "Project Sponsor's Responsibility" sections above).

If the Project Sponsor and Project Manager have done a good job of setting expectations and educating the Steering Committee and other executive stakeholders on Project Plan changes over time, then presenting changes due to the Project Integration Session results will likely be easier. That said, no matter how much preparation and good management has taken place, executives never like to hear that the schedule has been delayed, costs have increased, or the scope needs to be scaled back.

Ongoing Project Team Management

The Project Manager has two major responsibilities in managing the transformation. The first is to stay on top of the Project Plan as described above in this chapter. The second is to manage the Project Team staff throughout the time of the project. If you are reading this book as a Project Manager of a major transformation, read Chapter 5 (Build a High-Performing Transformation Project Team) twice!

You will be spending more of your time managing your people than doing any other task. It is a unique people management assignment because your team is temporary—and likely quite diverse. They will be from different departments and functions in the organization, and many might be consultants and contractors. You will have a brief period of time in which to get the team performing effectively and, throughout the life of the project, will be managing unique situations within the team that other managers do not have to face. For instance, do all of your team members who are full-time employees have a secure position to return to when they complete their project assignment? How do you keep energy up in a team that will likely be working long hours for long periods of time in a lengthy transformation project? Organizations should invest in providing their prime Transformation Project Manager candidates with effective project team management training to help them prepare for these unique situations.

CHAPTER 9

Step 9: Prepare for and Support the Transformation Launch

So most astronauts getting ready to lift off are excited and very anxious and worried about that explosion—because if something goes wrong in the first seconds of launch, there's not very much you can do.

—Sally Ride

My Step 9 Story:
You Can Never Be Too Prepared

We were three weeks before the launch of the first phase of a major organizational transformation within a large government-sector organization. The impact to employees was going to be very significant, including the announcement of major business process changes, organizational structure changes, and changes to individuals' roles. Some changes required people to changes locations and even reapply for newly created positions. The launch consisted of a series of carefully timed communications to individuals whose jobs were changing, then presentations to functional groups within the division, and finally a full division-wide formal presentation of all changes. I was the Program Manager of this transformation, reporting to an executive lead.

Our Steering Committee consisted of the full executive committee of the organization, and everyone was nervous about the launch. We realized that although a lot of the changes would be positive and welcomed, some individuals would not be happy with the changes to their jobs. There was a perceived lack of security, and there was a lot that could go wrong with the logistics of how changes were communicated. To allay the fears of the Steering Committee, and to better prepare for managing all aspects of this complex coordination, I prepared a detailed communication plan leading up to and following the announcements of the changes. These were the major parts of that plan:

Devise a detailed communication and logistics plan   Our Team created a well-timed and well-coordinated plan that required hour-by-hour planning of announcements and support to all employees. We needed to ensure that individuals whose roles were significantly changed were communicated with first. Supervisors had to be told of changes to their roles before their direct reports were, and it all had to be done quickly so no rumours spread before we could announce changes publicly. Each Team member and senior manager was assigned a role to speak to individuals so that everyone affected was covered. Human Resources had to prepare formal notices for all individuals affected by job changes. A large town hall meeting was organized for the day after all individuals and specific functional groups had been spoken to. Town hall communications had to be developed for all senior managers to present all changes. Finally, company-wide communication had to be developed to inform the rest of the organization of the changes that occurred. Every activity was assigned to a Team member accountable for completing each activity. We reviewed the plan as a whole team numerous times to ensure we didn't miss anything. Then we conducted dress rehearsals to practise our delivery. All of this may sound like overkill, but we were very serious about making no mistakes and ensuring that every individual was properly, accurately, and respectfully communicated to about their changing role in the organization and that the right supports were in place. We understood that even a small breach in communication protocol could result in a loss of confidence and trust in management, resulting in a poor adoption of the change.

Managing and reporting progress of the launch To ensure that the Executive Steering Committee was well informed, I created a very detailed plan in calendar format for the two-week period in which all communication would occur. It showed which activities took place on a daily, and even hourly, basis. In the last month, I was reporting weekly to the Steering Committee on these changes; in the last week, the day of, and two days after the launch, I reported daily. The week before the launch, our core internal Team had daily early-morning meetings, followed by a mid-day review by Change Champions and an end-of-day report to the Steering Committee. The union was also part of the communication plan, receiving notices of employee role changes early. Any changes or glitches were handled and communicated in real time.

As expected, there were a few individuals who were not happy or were very nervous about the changes that affected them. However, all individuals were well supported, and communication and timing of events went well. We didn't expect to receive praise for how well we managed the launch. This was a situation where things either went smoothly and we retained the trust and confidence built up over the course of the project or employees got angry and we lost that confidence and trust. The result of this intricate and extensive planning was a smooth launch, where the focus was on support and continuous communication.

Step 9 Activities

This Step addresses the final weeks before the transformation solution is launched and a few weeks past the go-live date. It includes the final testing, training, and launching of the solution and the period directly after the solution when the Project Team is still offering full project support. It also marks the most significant period of transition and change for the Project Team and the organization. During this period of the project, the Project Team will be preparing to transition from an intensive project activity schedule to a time of disbanding and ceasing to exist as a team. It is often the most challenging period for the Project Manager to lead the Project Team since he or she must keep the throttle on full while Team members will be thinking about, and perhaps be concerned about, what comes next for them. This Step outlines key activities to address all of these challenges.

It is important to note that this is the first step that deals with the period when the transformation or change takes place. This is appropriate because most of the work done to achieve a successful transformation is done before anything changes. If the foundation is not set and a critical mass of support is not created, then the solution will fail before it is even introduced. However, these last two steps are still critical and where the real change occurs.

The Transformation Project Launch is the date the transformation 'goes live.' In a technology project, it is when the new system goes live and is operational to all users. In a process transformation, it is when new processes are live and operational. In an organizational restructuring or merger, it is when all individuals begin formally operating in their new roles. The following steps are all essential in preparing for and supporting the Transformation Project Launch.

LAST STOP POINT IN 10-STEP PLAN

There are no more STOP POINTS in your transformation work after Step 9. Once your new solution is launched, it will be either a success or a failure. Whether it is a new IT system, a new set of processes, a changed organizational structure, or a new organizational strategy creating change, the new solution is now live.

Although minor adjustments or fixes are to be expected, if the solution is not adopted or does not work, it will be deemed a failure. Up to this point, any major problems are project problems or a project failure. After the launch, they are Project Launch failures and the only options are to go back to the old way of doing things or operate ineffectively and at a greater cost until a new or modified solution is developed. More damaging is the effect a failure could have on your customers if a loss of service or production is experienced. Since these are strategic projects and large in scope, these scenarios could cause a significant loss for the organization, or the company could even fail.

For this reason, the first nine steps of the 10-Step methodology deal with the organization doing everything it can to provide a number of checkpoints where the transformation project can be stopped before the wrong solution or a lack of preparation can cause real failure. The Project Sponsor and Executive Steering Committee must not succumb to the phenomenon of "escalation of commitment."[1] This phenomenon states that an individual (or individuals) will increasingly feel tied to an action or decision the greater the investment (time, money, and resources).

I have experienced many situations where it seemed prudent or even obvious to stop or cancel a large project, but so much time and money had been invested by that decision point that all executive leaders were afraid or unwilling to take this drastic action. There is a face-saving element to escalation of commitment as well, and a perception that an executive's career or career progression could be in jeopardy if the project doesn't proceed. If you find yourself in that executive position, think of how much more your career or career progression would be in jeopardy if you didn't stop when you could and instead the Project Launch was a failure. This is why it's so critical to get Step 1 right and so critical that the executive group be truly committed and have skin in the game for the success or failure of the project.

---

1   Barry Staw, "Knee-Deep in the Big Muddy: A Study of Escalating Commitment to a Chosen Course of Action," *Organizational Behaviour and Human Performance* 16:1 (June 1976): 27–44. Also at: http://strategy.sjsu.edu/www.stable/pdf/Staw,%20B%20M,%201976,%20Organizational%20Behavior%20and%20Human%20Performance.%2016%20pp%2027-44.pdf.

The whole executive group must understand that if the project must be stopped, the cost of doing so will never be as great as the cost of going live and of failure.

Testing and Acceptance of New Processes and Technology by Affected Stakeholders

All transformation solutions should test that the solution works before it is launched into the everyday operations of the organization. Technology Teams are typically the best and most comprehensive in their testing activities leading up to a launch. IT professionals have developed a very rigorous set of tests to make sure the technology and acceptance of the solution works (although the final set of tests, called User Acceptance Testing, is sometimes not executed well). For new processes, or other non-technology transformations, it is strongly recommended that the Project Team conduct a simulated solution demonstration.

CONDUCT SOLUTION SIMULATIONS FOR NON-TECHNOLOGY TRANSFORMATION PROJECTS

In many transformation projects, the simulation is called 'a day in the life' of the solution. The Project Manager directs its creation, and the simulation should be presented to all Functional Leaders who are accountable for managing key parts of the organization affected by the transformation.[2]

The Project Manager tasks the Team with creating a real-life simulation of how the new process or business operation

---

2   It is good practice to verify Project Steering Committee attendees for the simulation. This will ensure coverage and comprehensive representation for acceptance and sign-off on the solution before you go live.

will work when the transformation is operational. Using real business processes with real data, it demonstrates how all of the new changes will work. It emphasizes all changes to work tasks and activities, including:

- current work that will no longer be done

- current work that will be modified

- new work

New measures for success are identified and emphasized, and new ways of working or cultural changes are reviewed. If applicable, a schedule for implementation is reviewed (transformation solutions are often implemented in phases).

Finally, any issues and remaining risks must be openly stated and discussed.

Obtain Stakeholder Acceptance to Launch the Transformation

After the simulation and discussion are completed, the Project Manager formally asks for acceptance and sign-off on the solution. Acceptance and sign-off means that each stakeholder has confidence on two fronts: the solution is ready to go live in everyday business operations and the organization and their function are ready to perform the work differently as designed. Readiness means that:

- all stakeholders have been trained in new skills as required

- coaching and support is adequate in the short term as employees learn to become proficient in these new skills

- a critical mass of support for the solution has been achieved

- new processes are ready to go

- all previous major issues or concerns have been addressed (either resolved or an acceptable plan for resolution developed)

Acceptance and sign-off should be as formal as required and appropriate within the organization. Find out how other major successful business changes were accepted and agreed to, and use that approach.

ACHIEVE USER ACCEPTANCE FOR TECHNOLOGY TRANSFORMATIONS

There is a much more formal and extensive testing process required for technology transformation projects. Testing occurs on many different levels and for different reasons. Although all these tests are essential before launching a solution that works and is effective, only User Acceptance Testing (commonly known as UAT) will be addressed.

NON-TRANSFORMATION WORK

The 10-Step methodology will not cover the multiple kinds of technical testing that need to occur in a technology transformation. These other tests are the technical work that needs to be done for the solution to work but are not activities that address helping the organization develop support and commitment for the transformation solution. Other kinds of testing done for technology transformation include these tests, typically conducted in ERP implementations:

- Component Testing

- Configuration Testing

- Application Testing

- Conversion Testing

- Integration Testing

It is important that the Project Manager understands and coordinates these technical testing activities, usually through the leadership of a Technical Testing Lead. It is also important that the timing and dependencies are fully understood by the Team since they make up a key part of the Critical Path of the project.

User Acceptance Testing (UAT)

The objective of UAT is to raise users' confidence in the quality of the transformation solution so that they are able to sign off on it before going live. Since UAT is the last piece of testing done (it usually comes right before training), there is often pressure to compress the time to deliver it. Also, UAT requires a considerable amount of time from subject-matter expert stakeholders, who have likely been consulted with frequently during the course of designing the solution. 'Project fatigue' often occurs near the end of the project with these key resources required for UAT. However, it is important that the Project Manager not succumb to pressure to minimize or compress testing or to not involve the ideal group of subject-matter experts in UAT activities.

The schedule and resources required for UAT should be presented as early as possible to senior stakeholders to gain the necessary commitment for the time and resources required to complete this essential activity. The Project Manager should ensure that the following key principles are included in UAT activities:

Provide participants with adequate training to conduct the test
One of the biggest participant complaints about UAT is not receiving adequate training to effectively conduct the test or fully understand what they are testing. The Training Lead must be accountable for building in an early stream of training for all those identified as UAT participants. A good tactic is to identify Super Users very early in the project, train them first, involve them in early project development activities, and then use them in UAT.

Assume errors and issues will be found These will require modification and retesting. Ensure enough time is built into the plan to both conduct UAT and allow for adjustments to issues and errors that are discovered.

Provide proper context for what participants are testing This can be provided in training and then reiterated in UAT sessions. A UAT session should not be merely an instruction from the UAT Project Lead to "test whether 'X' function works by entering 'Y' keystrokes, and if 'Z' does not appear, enter 'error' for 'X' function." Instead, users should be provided with the context of what they are testing. They should be given enough information so that they can test their own scenarios.

Arrange coaching for participants The UAT project facilitator should coach individuals throughout their UAT experience to ensure they do not get stuck. Even with some training, participants should still not expect to be proficient in using the new technology. Also, something may not be working properly.

Allow participants to evaluate the solution on qualitative areas Feedback on ease of use, increased or enhanced functionality, or other non-technical areas will provide a broader assessment of whether the solution will be accepted and adopted by the general population. Some UAT activities focus only on whether the solution works as it is designed. That assessment alone will not necessarily identify opinions from participant users on whether the system will be readily adopted by the broader user community.

Aim for minimal or no surprises Most importantly, UAT should offer few surprises to participants. Ideally, participants will be subject-matter experts who have been involved throughout the solution design process, so their opinions would have been built into, and tested in, small pieces all along.[3]

At the end of UAT, participants must formally accept the solution as ready and acceptable to launch.

NOTE: UAT participants must understand that they have been hand-picked to represent their function of the business to formally sign off acceptance of the technology solution. They must feel comfortable in this role, and the UAT facilitator should encourage them to raise their hand if anything is not understood or if they see any issues in what they are testing.

---

3   Project Managers leading technology transformation projects would benefit from understanding tactics and techniques used in Agile Project Management for working with the user community to develop support. Agile is a method developed originally to manage the design of new systems and relies heavily on the continuous and frequent feedback from and acceptance of users for all functionality developed by the Project Team. This tactic will pay big dividends and help 'load the dice' in achieving sign-off in final UAT.

If participants do not sign off on UAT, the project is officially on hold until they do. If stakeholders and these participants have been involved as recommended in previous steps, then an actual project stoppage is unlikely. However, it is possible, or even expected, for something new to pop up, or for errors or issues that need resolution to be identified. Therefore, it would be prudent for the Project Manager to build a contingency for problems and error resolution into UAT activities, which will lengthen the Critical Path and launch date.

Train All Internal and External Stakeholders on New Processes and Technology

Until it begins, stakeholders often view training as a necessary support activity. Initially, they are more focused on the solution and how it will affect their role and their work. Once training begins, however, all eyes are on how well it is conducted and received. Poorly conducted training can cause enough concern to delay the launch of a transformation project. Therefore, the Project Manager must ensure that the Team delivers effective, high-quality training.

Chapter 3 (Design and Manage Effective Training and Communication Activities) covered all the elements that are required to develop and deliver a training plan. The following are some more detailed points for the Project Manager and the Training Lead to consider when actually delivering the training to the stakeholders who require it.

TRAINING PREPARATION

A significant amount of administrative coordination needs to begin several weeks before training occurs. The following activities need to be initiated and managed up to and throughout training delivery activities.

Develop and maintain a comprehensive, accurate list of all stakeholders requiring training   One of the more challenging administrative items to manage is identifying and maintaining an accurate list of stakeholders for your transformation project. You would think that this would be easy—just identify every function that is affected and find out what roles are affected, then go to Human Resources (HR) and get an accurate list of the individuals in those roles. You would assume that since HR handles payroll, the list would be correct. For technology transformations, this should also be easy: simply get a list of all users who have access on the current legacy systems and that should yield a comprehensive list. However, many organizations have inaccurate lists of employees matched to their roles. One reason for this is that managers tend to move people around and then forget to update Human Resources records on role assignments. Other reasons are inaccurate or faulty legacy systems and issues related to other administrative processes. Often, system access is updated, and users don't formally have the proper access they need to do their jobs, so they create ways to get around the errors (such as having other people sign on or sharing work tasks).

The only way to ensure your list is accurate is to go to your managers and find out who all of the stakeholders/users are. It is a lengthy process initially, but if you don't do it, you can expect to miss people and/or improperly assign training. There must also be a process put in place for updating this list, either regularly or at least once just before training invitations are sent out. The Training Lead or Project Coordinator could monitor this task.

If Human Resources and other executives insist that their records are accurate, and that this will be a wasteful and unnecessary use of project resources, present this point to the Steering Committee for a full executive sign-off. I have seen more than one transformation project derailed because the Project Team discovered at the eleventh hour that employee lists were inaccurate.

Provide at least three to four weeks' notice of training to all participants Employees need time to manage their schedule. They also want to have confidence that training is planned and under control. The less notice you provide to people to attend training, the greater the chance you will have people rejecting invitation notices or just not showing up.

Communicate training as mandatory You are providing training for a strategic transformation solution of the highest priority for the organization. For it to be successful, people being trained need to be trained on how to work differently. It should be made clear that this is essential training that everyone must attend as part of their job contract. The message that training is mandatory should be sent from the highest level of the organization (the CEO if he or she is the crossover manager, or whoever is in that role), and reinforced by managers of each function.

Communicate key details of the training Information builds trust in participants that the training is well planned, rich in subject matter, and worthwhile. Beyond the basics of time, location, and other logistics, include such items as instructor information, context and content of training, and a feedback mechanism for questions.

Arrange Help Desk training (for technology transformations) Support and preparation for the IT Help Desk is often omitted or inadequately provided. The Help Desk will usually be the first point of contact for new users on new technology. Support, confidence, and ultimately adoption will be in jeopardy if the Help Desk staff are not properly prepared. The following are suggested activities to address this need:

- Develop customized training on how to document, respond to, and direct questions to the right place in readiness for the launch of the technology solution. Build this into your training plan, and for maximum retention, deliver it around the same time as training is delivered to other users.

- Create redirected routing of Help Desk calls for users who have queries on any new technology. This technique is commonly used when the Help Desk may need more time to get up to speed and/or when there are specific issues that require delicate handling in the first few weeks of the launch. Typically, users hear an additional option number presented when they first call the Help Desk; when pressed, users are directed to a technology solution specialist you have assigned to handle queries (usually a Project Team solution expert).

TRAINING DELIVERY

Follow the advice outlined in Chapter 3 (Design and Manage Effective Training and Communication Activities). Below are additional tips to help make your training activities effective.

Build in contingency for schedule changes Unforeseen organizational or external events may cause training to be rescheduled. For example, flu season could cause absences that require follow-up training sessions.

Assign back-up instructors One significant risk that Project Managers often do not think of is the sudden loss of the only instructor able to deliver a portion of training. This is an unacceptable resource risk that can be mitigated by doubling up or overlapping training. Ensure that there is one back-up person for every key aspect of training that must be delivered before the go-live date.

Encourage practice and offer support during training Communicate details for how to practise new skills, and post go-live coaching and support during training. As discussed in Step 3, even the best training will not make participants expert or even proficient in their new skills.

Conduct evaluations These can be done in class or online directly after class (there will be better uptake during class). Evaluations should be done to validate the quality of training, to assess the success of the learning experience, and to gather feedback on how to continuously improve the learning experience in future sessions or changes.

Avoid scheduling training in the summer months   Vacation time spikes very high in the months of June, July, and August— called the dead zone by many Project Training Leads. If training has to happen in these months, you need to build in extra time for makeup classes to train those people who were away on vacation.

PRACTICE

Step 3 described the importance of allowing people to practise their new skills without the fear of making mistakes. It might be in a simulated workspace created for learners or in a more formal training sandbox for technology transformations. Communicate the details for how and when training participants can access this practice space. Encourage people to practise, and make access and use of the practice space easy and accommodating. Provide contact information for learners if they experience any difficulties accessing or using the practice space or if they get stuck at any point while practising.

Set Up Success Measures

Before launching the transformation solution, the Project Manager and Project Sponsor must identify a set of transformation solution performance measures that will comprehensively and effectively measure how successful the transformation is in the short and long term. These measures are a quantification of your original compelling business case, when you stated: "If we don't change 'X' by 'Y' time, then an unacceptable 'Z' will happen."

Measures must be congruent with, or the same as, the measures that the Executive Team already regularly tracks to assess the organization's health. These are the performance measures that will tell the organization whether the solution has been successful in the long term. Think of your organization as a large ship, the transformation as a new route, and these macro measures as the new port of call. Typically, these measures are one or more of the following:

- increase of productivity efficiency or effectiveness

- decrease of total business costs

- increase of sales or market share

Once identified, medium- and long-term time goals should be validated. The Project Sponsor should ensure that the Steering Committee and Executive Team are aware of the productivity dip that should initially be expected in the short term, while the organization adjusts to the change. A baseline measure should be taken at the launch, and these measures should be assessed at three- and six-month intervals.

The Project Manager and Project Sponsor should also identify more specific measures that indicate how well the technology, process, and people changes are working so that adjustments can be made if required. Think of these 'micro' measures as your navigation system to keep you on course and the many minor adjustments you need to make as the helm, responding to tides, currents, winds ... or even the occasional storm!

Create a plan for operationalizing the collecting of data. Attempt to identify macro and micro data that is already being collected, but prepare for the fact that some data will create work for areas such as business analysts or the Help Desk (in technology transformations).

Manage Transformation Launch Week

Regardless of what kind of transformation is being managed, the final week of the project, during which the transformation is launched, must be managed very tightly. For most of the preparation time during the project, it is sufficient to manage issues and communicate important elements of the transformation project on a weekly basis. During the last month or few weeks, the Project Manager should move into daily management mode, and the last week should be managed on almost an hourly basis or close to real time. Here are some recommendations for how that final week should be managed.

Create a Command Centre   The Project Manager, key Project Leads, and potentially one or two key stakeholders form this core group to manage activities for the week.

Place Project Team Leads and Team members at key locations on-site among stakeholders   For technology transformation, coaches should be assigned who will visit users' desks to help them when they get stuck. Determine a plan that will give stakeholders maximum real-time, on-site support for the first week or two that the solution goes live. 'Coach the coaches' on how to provide service so it is professional and consistent at every location.

CREATE A DAILY COMMUNICATION SCHEDULE FOR LAUNCH WEEK

A set of three meetings daily may seem onerous for launch week, but it will keep executive stakeholders and other key people aware and informed. Be sure to keep the meetings brief and focused on the specific objective for each.

Early-morning Command Centre meeting   Update the status of yesterday's issues and discuss new issues for today. Ensure everything is on track. This meeting should last twenty to thirty minutes maximum and be facilitated by the Project Manager.

Mid-day Change Champion meeting   Update the Change Champion Committee on any issues, and find out whether new issues have arisen in any specific functions. This meeting should last twenty to thirty minutes maximum and be facilitated by the Project Manager.

End-of-Day Steering Committee phone call   The Steering Committee should be provided with a brief update on Project Launch status, mainly to give these executives confidence that everything is on track and to report on any issues so there are no surprises. This meeting (typically a conference call) should last no more than ten to fifteen minutes and be facilitated by the Project Sponsor (with the Project Manager in attendance). The Project Manager and the Team will follow up on managing issues in real time after each of these meetings.

SAMPLE MEETING SCHEDULE FOR TRANSFORMATION LAUNCH WEEK

From my experience with large-scale transformations, starting your launch-week countdown on a Friday and going live on the following Wednesday has one big advantage: if a serious last-minute issue arises and requires time to resolve it, the Project Team will be able to address it over the weekend. With that timeline in mind, this is the recommended schedule to manage the daily meetings:

On the Friday, Monday, and Tuesday before the launch date Conduct the daily meetings as proposed above.

On the day of the launch (Wednesday) Have the same daily meetings but ensure that they are very brief and held via telephone conference call instead of in-person. The Project Manager, Project Team, and Change Champions should all spend their time walking the floor and supporting stakeholders and observing how things are working. Oftentimes, the day of the launch is like being in the eye of the storm: things will appear to be very calm, with few issues. It usually takes a day or two for issues or problems to surface.

On Thursday and Friday after the launch Return to your regular daily meeting schedule. The Change Champion Committee and Steering Committee can decide on Friday whether there is a need and desire to continue with the meeting schedule on the following Monday. If things are going well, the mid-day and end-of-day meetings will stop.

Continue your daily early-morning Command Centre meetings for another week There will be other issues, and assume you are still in real-time support mode. The Project Manager will make a decision on the following Friday if these meetings need to continue for another few days or weeks.

Project Team Support for Two to Four Weeks Post-Launch

No matter how good the training was or how much practice time employees put into learning new skills required to use new systems and conduct new work tasks, they will not be proficient in using new technologies or completing new work processes when the transformation solution first goes live. Employees will rely on having a lot of support for a period of time, until adequate proficiency is developed. The productivity curve often looks like this:

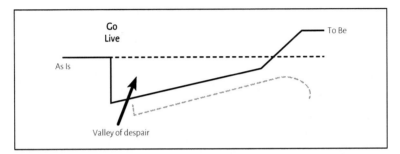

FIGURE 6. **Productivity curve after the transformation launch**

The solid black line shows a level of productivity before the change, a dip after launch, and then a faster rate of growth in productivity that overtakes the pre-launch rate and reaches a higher norm. If intensive project support is not provided and people don't feel supported, the dashed grey line shows what might result: slow growth that never reaches pre-launch productivity levels and either evens out at lower rates or drops again—or the organization may stay in the zone indicated as the 'Valley of Despair.'

The dip in productivity is inevitable after the launch of a major organizational solution. What may differ between organizations is the length of time it takes for productivity to move back up and the level it achieves in establishing a new productivity norm.

All the preparation in Steps 1 through 9 will have helped the organization move on the black-line path of speedier and more effective productivity growth. To kick-start this faster growth, one of the most important activities is for the Project Team to offer intensive project support and coaching through at least the first few weeks after the project solution is launched. This is certainly required immediately after the launch of a technology transformation. Stakeholders may feel lost, not knowing who to turn to the moment the technology solution is live. The extent to which this post-launch support is required, and for how long, may vary in other types of organizational transformations.

ASSIGN AND PREPARE ON-SITE COACHES

The Project Team specialists who helped develop the transformation solution or who are expert or knowledgeable about it are ideal candidates to be on-site coaches. For many technology transformations, the term 'Super User' is used for this coaching role. (Super Users are hand-selected individuals from areas highly impacted by the change who are trained early and more in depth. Their role is to act as coaches among their peers when the change is launched. See also Chapter 3 for a fuller description of Super Users.) As the Project Manager, you will certainly need an 'all hands on deck' approach to assigning coaches since you will want as much face-to-face, real-time coverage as possible.

In a large, multi-location organization, you will need to devise a schedule with Project Team coaches assigned 'coaching stations'; they may need to travel around (floor to floor or building to building) to ensure there is at least some daily physical coverage for all stakeholders. If this is required, publish a schedule that is communicated to all stakeholders before the launch.

Assign coaches or Super Users to coaching stations in the working area of their peers, to work alongside Project Team specialist coaches.

Conduct preparatory sessions for Project Team specialists and Super Users/coaches to ensure there is a consistent service approach to coaching all stakeholders and that all coaching preparations, materials, and logistics are understood. Review key issues that could be expected according to the most recent stakeholder feedback from training and other feedback mechanisms.

DEVELOP ENHANCED TELEPHONE AND/OR EMAIL SUPPORT

Often, Project Teams of technology launches only provide email contacts to stakeholders who ask for assistance. Although costly and a challenge to resources, it pays big dividends to also provide voice support if no direct phone option to a Help Desk exists. Multiple options for assistance not only provide a greater perception of a 'blanket of support' for users but also disperse calls to more than one source for help. Targeted contacts are very good if it makes sense and can be resourced (target contacts are assigned contacts for specific content areas of the solutions or types of issues).

At the very least, provide detailed content support lists for on-site coaches and Super Users to enable a more targeted and quicker response to queries.

PROVIDE ON-SITE/AT-DESK SUPPORT POST-LAUNCH

Enhanced on-site/at-desk support should be provided for at least two to four weeks after the launch to get stakeholders 'over the hump' while they are building up proficiency in new processes and technology. One good approach is a graduated lessening of support over several weeks.

In my experience, support activity is rarely allotted enough time. Often, after only a few days of intensive support from the Project Team and/or solution experts, it abruptly ends. This frequently causes anxiety and many situations where staff get stuck on their new work tasks. The best approach is a gradual lifting of support over a longer period of time.

I once listened to a show on parenting, and the expert characterized parenting as "the art and science of 'letting go.'" The message was that parents must decide when to begin giving their children more and more freedom to make decisions and to be on their own, with appropriate guidance—but always with the understanding and goal of having each child become a totally independent and capable adult. Although organizations are not supporting children through their transformations, it struck me that the concept is similar. Staff begin major changes in their work with the need for full support. As organizational leaders, your job is to support them, with the goal of helping them move to competent independence.

Celebrate Project Closure

A separate Project Team celebration event should occur when most core Team members are still with the project. This provides an opportunity for the Project Sponsor and Project Team to formally both recognize and celebrate the Project Team's achievements. Timing for this kind of event is always challenging, since the ideal time is a few weeks before the Team disbands, which would be right in the middle of your

Project Launch. Timing for this event could be as early as just before the launch to sometime after the launch. It is more meaningful for Team members to have this event before the Team disbands and would help infuse energy into the Project Team's post-launch support activities.

CHAPTER 10

Step 10: Sustain the Transformation – Create the New Norm

When there is a contradiction between what the organization says it wants employees to do and how employees are rewarded for their work, employees will ignore what they are being told and will do what they are rewarded for ... every time.

—A truth I've come to know

My Step 10 Story: Asking for A and Rewarding for B Always Gets You B

Many years ago, I was an internal Program Manager for a quality improvement initiative in a major chemical organization that manufactured paint for cars. The work of managing the project followed the first nine steps fairly comprehensively. The rationale for the change was that the organization was losing traction in the marketplace as competitors raised the bar in their quality standards. It was the 1980s, and Quality Management was all the rage, instigated by Japanese manufacturers who were significantly beating North American manufacturers in producing high-quality products. Good evidence was presented and executives were on board to make major changes in production practices that put quality ahead of schedule.

An effective plan was put in place to develop specific process solutions, prepare the organization, and then test, train, and launch these new ways of working. Training and communication were consistently rated highly by the majority of participants. At the time of the launch, things appeared to go quite well, and early adoption metrics were very good. People understood and were using the new techniques, and after a very short downward blip in production (which was expected), quality figures started to rise.

However, after several months, inexplicable drops in quality started appearing in several plants. This made no sense to me or anyone else. After talking to supervisors and employees on the production floor, I found the problem fairly quickly. The culture was one that valued meeting the schedule as the number-one priority.

The plant made chemical liquid coatings for the automobile industry, and on the production floor they used to have a saying: "If it flows, it goes." The new production methods tried to change this culture by telling employees that the number-one priority was now quality: "If the product is substandard or you see a problem on the line, stop production." Every employee was told that he or she was empowered to stop the line if they saw a flaw. Initially, things went well because employees were motivated to try new techniques and liked the idea that they had this new authority, responsibility, and respect. So what changed?

More to the point: what didn't change? Monetary and other incentives were not changed to align with new quality-priority production techniques. Supervisors and employees were still given incentives to get the product out on time. Shipping supervisors and employees were still receiving pressure from customers to meet delivery schedules, and senior management were not properly reinforcing new quality measures. Long-term incentives were discussed and recommended at the outset of the change but were not put in place or truly enacted by senior management. The end result? Production culture started reverting back to its old number-one priority.

Interestingly, after I presented my findings on what was causing this quality slippage, the executives debated what they should do about it. It seemed that it wasn't until this moment that we uncovered some latent resistance at the executive level for truly moving to a 'quality-first' organization. Many—especially the VP of sales—were more nervous about changing the priority than they originally let on. During a session I facilitated, it was clear that the VP still believed that the majority of the company's tier-1 customers still valued the schedule as their number-one priority ... and that the company would lose customers if their schedule metrics slipped. It was better to beat everyone on schedule and simply replace product if it was substandard. At least they would not jeopardize losing accounts. He was describing the old culture—the one this transformation was supposed to replace.

The quality-improvement philosophy holds that once staff became proficient at new production techniques, the schedule would improve. In the end, a compromised, phased-in approach was adopted, with tighter controls on stopping production. The company also modified its reward systems to include more product-quality metrics. The moral of the story is: before you launch your change, your organization needs to understand what its current business culture is and then determine what reward practices it needs to change to entrench a new culture.

Step 10 Activities

During the first several weeks after the change is operational, the organization should spend most of its time making sure the solution works. Fix glitches and issues, and make sure people are supported on many levels so that production and service levels aren't adversely affected while everyone gets up to speed.

Moving from the 'Honeymoon' to Struggling with Change

Right after the change goes live is a hectic time for the Project Team and for the senior stakeholders who are trying to support their staff while still getting work done. At first, the change will be a novelty and should spark a lot of initial interest and curiosity. People will check it out. Use this initial interest as an opportunity to gain true longer-term support, but do not make the mistake of believing this initial interest and activity will provide any indication of true adoption of the transformation. It usually is an artificial 'honeymoon' period.

Expect enthusiasm to decrease when the dust settles after the launch of your change. If you could plot an 'enthusiasm curve' for affected stakeholders regarding a new strategic change, it would look like this:

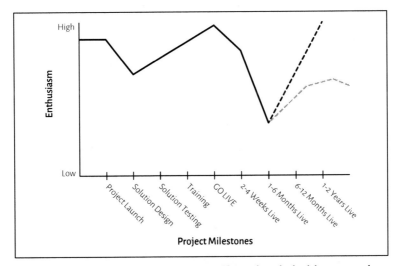

FIGURE 7. Enthusiasm curve among affected stakeholders over the course of a strategic change

Enthusiasm will be fairly high at Project Launch, decrease somewhat during Solution Design, be very high at go-live, begin to fall a little a few weeks after launch, and fall to its lowest level early in the first one to six months. At this point, response typically diverges. The black dotted line shows enthusiasm rising more quickly, reaching launch levels by month three, while the grey dotted line rises more slowly and never reaches that high level.

There are many reasons why enthusiasm will begin to wane after the first month of implementing a large change, including these three main ones:

Reason #1: Initial novelty of the change wears off   Curiosity seekers will have checked out the new solution, and only those who need to conduct new tasks to do their job will continue to be active users or supporters.

Reason #2: Intensive support from the Project Team stops   When that happens, many stakeholders will not yet be totally proficient in their new skills and tasks. People will need time to gain the same proficiency they had in the old systems, processes, and roles. This is an uncomfortable place for people to be. Regardless of how good the initial Project Team support was during the first few weeks of the change, stakeholders/users will need to figure things out for themselves with less support.

Reason #3: New resistance often appears   After deeper understanding of the effect of the change sinks in, their commitment to it may change. No matter how good the Project Team and Functional Leaders were in preparing individuals for the change, the light bulb often will not go on for employees affected by the change until they become more proficient and are regularly applying their new skills. Once they understand what their role really is, how difficult or easy tasks are to complete, how interesting the work is, and what the new volume of work is, the reaction could be positive, neutral, or negative. A lot of other change management theories or methodologies state that the Project Team must determine the WIIFMs (What's In It For Me) during an early comprehensive stakeholder analysis preparation phase (Steps 6 and 7). This early analysis will uncover a lot of resistance, but expect new resistance to occur after people are using their new skills and conducting new tasks after the transformation is launched.

As a Project Manager, Project Sponsor, or Change Leader, your job is to manage the change effectively so that your organization takes the path of the black dotted line in the graph above.

At the beginning of the project, although business leaders know they ultimately own the change, in reality they are almost totally reliant on the Project Team to tell them what to do. They cannot drive the change because they don't yet understand it. While the solution is being developed, the Project Sponsor and Project Manager have been communicating with and involving the business leaders who will own the change, building their understanding and confidence in managing the change themselves. After training, the Project Manager must start to provide more opportunities for business leaders who own the processes that will be most affected by change, to start directing activities and driving change themselves. By the time the launch occurs, the only real accountability that the Project Team should have is providing training and coaching support to all those who need it and conducting solution adjustments and fixes if required. The business leaders who own the change should be fully driving the change at this point. It is the business leaders who must deal with the real challenges that come with a major transformation.

Begin Collecting and Assessing Performance Data

From the moment the transformation solution goes live, data should be collected according to the plan set out in Step 9.

Soon after the transformation launch, 90% to 95% of the stakeholders affected should be working in the new transformation solution. For new technology, this would be the percentage of users provided access who log on to the system. User log-on measurements should be tempered with how often they are expected to go on the system. Some users would need to get on the system daily, while others may only need to log on weekly or at greater intervals. For new processes or other strategic changes, measuring usage requires investigation, perhaps by brief survey or assigning internal stakeholders to each function to report usage. This rate of usage may be called an early "adoption rate"[1] and is important to get as an initial measurement that the new solution is at least being accessed. Ideally, the percentage of early adoption should be 100% since old systems or processes should be turned off, but there are usually a few technical glitches in new systems or processes that require adjustment before 100% usage is achieved.

However, true long-term adoption typically means that stakeholders affected by the change are proficient and truly committed to the new way of operating.

Measures on proficiency can be assessed through the number and type of queries stakeholders ask their coaches and other support sources. In the first few weeks, expect a high number of calls and queries. Use this data as a baseline in the first several weeks of the new transformation launch.

Develop reports on process or systems errors. Expect errors to occur even after the most effective design, development, and testing work. Conditions may have changed, or scenarios

---

1   Definition of "adoption rate": The number of members of a society who start using a new technology or innovation during a specific period of time. The rate of adoption is a relative measure, meaning that the rate of one group is compared with the adoption rate of another, often of the entire society. From website: www.investopedia.com/terms/r/rate-of-adoption.asp.

that were untested may have uncovered flaws in the solution. Don't be afraid to make adjustments to technology, process, and people as required.

Transitioning from a Project to Normal Operations

After the first few weeks of intensive support to stakeholders, the Project Team will disband and employees will be left on their own to use their new skills and apply the new transformation solution. Many organizations quickly disband the Project Team and leave employees on their own, believing that the work of supporting them in applying their new skills is over. Remember that from the perspective of most employees and stakeholders, the change began at the time of launch. All the work done over the many prior months has not yet affected stakeholders.

The Project Team should stay in place for the first several weeks of the launch to work on transitioning management of the change to the natural leaders of the organization. If the Project Manager has followed *Big Change* Steps 1 through 9, then this transition will likely be a seamless process with only a few final hand-offs.

Conduct 'Lessons Learned' Focus Group Sessions

Although the Project Team disbands between four and eight weeks after the launch, either the Project Manager should briefly return or the current leader should undertake to hold focus groups or Q&A sessions on Lessons Learned. In the first several weeks, both the Project Team and affected stakeholders will be too busy getting used to the changes to focus on an exercise like this. Lessons Learned exercises identify what worked well and what could be improved in the Transformation Launch.

Create a Super User Community of Practice

Step 3 introduced the idea of selecting and training Super Users or subject-matter experts (SMEs). If the Project Manager followed the advice of Step 3, then a Super User Community of Practice (CoP) will already be operating. Before the project solution is launched, an expert CoP focuses its time on sharing experiences with the solution to build member skills and expertise. After the solution is launched, although the CoP will still share learnings to continually build its expertise, the focus should shift more to sharing techniques and strategies for getting other users/stakeholders up to speed and proficient more quickly. Before the Project Team disbands, the Project Manager can have a final session with the established CoP and recommend that the group consider:

- meeting at least monthly to share learnings and effective coaching techniques

- continuing operations for at least six to twelve months after the solution goes live

- assigning rotation of leadership every few months to keep energy and interest high without undue burden on any individual or group

- inviting solution experts from both internal and external sources to attend meetings for discussions on their areas of expertise to help identify ways to continuously improve the implementation of the new solution

- running 'lunch and learn' or other extra learning/coaching sessions on selected solution topics to help accelerate learning and proficiency, either for the general staff or for coaches on coaching tips and techniques

- assigning a Senior Stakeholder Leader as CoP Sponsor to allow costs and resources to be assigned as and when required

Manage Resistance after Go-Live

For any organization, identifying and dealing with resistance and indifference is perhaps the most difficult part of managing a major transformation. Techniques for dealing with this resistance or indifference are discussed in the previous nine steps. They are addressed again in this step because many individuals may only exhibit resistance after the change is live, when the real impact is understood or felt.

In the short term, good preparation, communication, and training can spur early compliance and enthusiasm for a change. In the long term, people are motivated to do what they are rewarded for.

Before the transformation goes live, the Project Manager should be putting a plan in place to assess formal and informal business culture in relation to current formal and informal rewards and reinforcements to ensure that they are congruent with the new change. The Project Manager must work with business leaders to find out, first, whether any contradictions exist in their organization's formal or informal business culture. (In my story above, there were significant contradictions in how employees and management reinforced employee behaviour through the incentives.) Then, they need to work with whomever controls the rewards and incentives to make adjustments that will help develop long-term, sustainable change.

Formal business culture rewards include pay-for-performance systems, bonus plans, profit-sharing plans, or any other formal financial reward system that the organization applies to all employees and that is tied to individual or group performance. The organization must scrutinize all its company-wide financial reward systems to check that the formula applied is congruent with the changes being implemented.

The Project Manager may conduct the initial work of Step 10, but follow-through and implementation will mostly be done by other leaders in the organization. The Project Manager must ensure that part of the transformation project's transition plan identifies a leader for assessing and adjusting business culture rewards and reinforcements. If the senior Human Resource executive reports to the CEO and sits at the executive table during strategic decision-making discussions, then that person is an option. Otherwise, the Project Sponsor or any other operational executive could step in as the driver of Step 10. The assigning of appropriate resources for required tasks would then become part of normal business operations.

Identify Changes and Impacts to Strategic Performance Measures

The best way to discover whether your change will impact your business culture is to see whether any of your organization's business performance metrics, or their priority, will change. In the example given in the Step 10 story, there were no new strategic performance measures, only a different prioritization and weighting of them. Ask the following questions in examining the impacts of these changes:

- Are any of the strategic measures being changed included in overall organizational performance measurements?

- Are these current organizational performance measurements part of the organization's employee bonus structure? Are these current organizational performance measures typically part of functional or individual performance objectives?

- Are any of the organizational performance measures that will be changed or modified by the transformation solution part of the "priority business culture driver"? A priority business culture driver is a priority measurement that drives work behaviour, priority decisions, and work activity. In other words, does your organization have one or two key business objective measurements that have the same effect as "if it flows, it goes"?

The key question to ask is the last one. Rephrased: Does the transformation require managers and employees to change their priority business culture driver(s)? If it does, the organization must be prepared to adjust key organizational performance measures to sustain the new business culture in the longer term.

The organization should not be looking to change the *system* of business culture rewards, only *what* is being rewarded.

REVIEW THE CURRENT REWARD SYSTEMS

In the first two to three months after the change is live, review the current reward systems. The goal is to assess whether there are any rewards in place that are contradictory to what should now be rewarded, or whether there may be opportunities to reward new behaviour or performance that is now important.

Identify all criteria used in the formula for monetary increases Include benefits, perks, or other tangible rewards provided by the organization as recognition of achieving performance targets.

Highlight quantitative performance measures affected by the transformation solution It is essential to include:

- factors that are now contradictory to new strategic goals and objectives

- factors that are given the wrong priority weighting for what is now a priority in the new strategic goals and objectives

Identify gaps What quantitative performance measures are missing from the formula?

Reset the formula for calculating rewards The objective is to:

- eliminate or reduce those factors that reinforce behaviour contradictory to new strategic direction

- add factors currently missing that reinforce behaviour and the business culture of the new strategic direction

- assess from an organizational, group, and individual perspective whether new formulas reward all equitably

(Performance reward systems are complicated things. Sometimes, a group reward that seems to make sense and reward the right thing may inadvertently treat individuals inequitably or unfairly. Create test scenarios at the individual, group, and organizational level to prevent this issue.)

IMPLEMENT THE ADJUSTED REWARD PLAN

The Productivity Curve (Chapter 9, Figure 6, page 167) and the Enthusiasm Curve (Chapter 10, Figure 7, page 177) illustrate the phenomenon of both productivity and enthusiasm dipping soon after implementing a major transformation. As discussed, these dips are risks to long-term adoption—risks that can be compounded by making changes to business culture reward systems too soon or by mistiming the announcement of changes.

Determine timing and strategy for introducing reward systems changes   If the majority of employees are within the dip of productivity or enthusiasm, the timing is not right: they will resent what they perceive as being penalized for going through the pain of change. To guard against a decrease in adoption:

- hold off on making changes until productivity and enthusiasm metrics have at least risen to the levels they were before the change

- communicate in advance what the changes will be, with the assurance of implementation only when proficiency and productivity levels have risen to a level where incentives have a positive effect. NOTE: This tactic emphasizes the importance of measuring results frequently and comprehensively during the first months of implementing the change. It also sends a strong message to employees that the organization is serious about supporting its employees through the transformation.

Communicate the changes   There are two ideal times and two inappropriate times to communicate changes in business culture rewards systems.

- Ideal Communication Time #1: Just before launch, when enthusiasm and productivity levels should still be high. Nothing has changed yet, so productivity levels should be at least at normal levels. In fact, an old proven organizational behaviour phenomenon called the "Hawthorne Effect" might have occurred, making production levels inexplicably higher than normal.[2]

- Ideal Communication Time #2: Several months after launch, when productivity and enthusiasm dips show a move back to at least a neutral position. If Steps 1 through 9 were followed and the transformation solution has proven to be the right one, this should occur

---

2   The Hawthorne Effect is a term coined from the results of a series of studies conducted in the 1920s at the Hawthorne Works, part of Western Electric Company, by Elton Mayo of Harvard University. Mayo was testing the effect on workers of changing working conditions (physical and social) at the plant. The results were unexpected and baffling. Productivity rose regardless of whether changes were negative or positive. Although the scientific methods of the Hawthorne studies have been criticized, most experts agree that workers increased their productivity simply because they knew the organization wanted them to and expected those results from the changes imposed. Schermerhorn Hunt Osborne, *Managing Organizational Behaviour* (Toronto: John Wiley & Sons, 1991), 556.

within the first two to three months of the launch. Employees will be ready to receive this information in a positive vein and not feel penalized, since productivity figures are now more positive.

- Inappropriate Communication Time #1: Within the first month after launch, when productivity and enthusiasm is likely at low levels. Employees will immediately calculate what impact the new formula will have on their performance pay and bonuses. It will likely be negative at current productivity levels. Although you can communicate to employees that they shouldn't worry and their levels will rise as their proficiency gets better, enthusiasm is likely low, so the message will not be positively received. Also, people will be concentrating on how to do things differently.

- Inappropriate Communication Time #2: If you communicate changes six months or more after the launch, adoption slippage may have already occurred. Employees will have become more proficient, but they also will have now had the time to realize the inconsistencies with the current business culture reward systems, and as a result many may have stopped supporting or using their new skills.

◾ ◾ ◾

There is a common belief among many executives and leaders that once a new solution is built and the old one is retired, employees will have no choice but to adopt the new system. This belief is most common in large strategic technology change. Although it seems logical and true, it is neither. To help prove that point, let's revisit the example I provided in the Introduction.

If you recall, while I was with CapGemini Ernst & Young in 2002, we were helping Bombardier launch their second attempt at implementing a large ERP/SAP project. In early discussions with the internal director of the project, he reviewed the history of the first failed attempt and told me that their goal had been to have ten thousand users up and running in two years, and that they had only managed two hundred users in that time. My obvious first question was: "What happened?" Followed by: "What do you attribute the failure to? Were there technical issues? Training issues? What are the specific reasons for failure?" At one point, the project director said: "We screwed up at the very beginning of the project. Consensus was achieved among the executive corporate team that the ERP solution was the right solution for the organization, and they were all quite excited on the direction we were taking. They gave the CIO the authority and mandate to implement the system throughout all the business divisions of the organizations. We believed that we had done our due diligence to achieve executive support for the change. We had not. Our organization is divided into several very large divisions that operate as separate companies. The presidents of each of those divisions are very autonomous in their operational decision-making. None of them was properly consulted with on the needs and benefits of the new system. All had issues with all or part of the solution. None of these presidents supported the ERP solution, and they communicated this to their staff. Needless to say, the Project Team motored on, and built, tested, and launched the solution."

The story is worth repeating, first, because it is the best extreme example of poor adoption of a major transformation solution that I have experienced and, second, because even after building a new system and decommissioning the old ones, users within all of the organization's divisions were still able to do their jobs without using the new system. How was that possible? In this case, many of the legacy systems were spreadsheets, and IT was not going to cancel licences for Excel. However, even when corporate IT stopped supporting other systems when the ERP system went live, the presidents of each division ensured that internal IT support was given the resources and funding to continue using those legacy systems. Although a radical response, organizations must understand that if adoption does not occur, employees and management will find a way to circumvent the new solution and either revert to their old legacy systems or find optional means to get their work done.

Adjust Informal Business Culture Rewards and Reinforcements

Informal business culture rewards and recognition are more difficult to both identify and change. A lot has been written on the Top 5 or Top 10 reasons for resistance in organizations.[3] Most of the research lists reasons and assigns them to all levels of the organization. While accurate and well examined, it does not address how resistance differs between levels of the organization.

Senior managers are usually on the receiving end of changes. Once they believe the transformation solution will work, it is typically not difficult for them to change. For example: In the implementation of a new ERP or Business Intelligence System, most executives are usually not very active users. They are typically the recipients of new reports that will now provide them with deeper and more meaningful information—support for the change is not a hard sell.

Front-line non-supervisory staff is much more affected by the change than senior management, but their concerns often focus on how they will learn and become proficient in new tasks.

In major organizational transformations, the most stubborn resistance is usually found at the middle management and front-line management levels.

Informal business culture rewards and recognition are non-monetary, awarded to employees by front-line managers and supervisors for a job well done. They range anywhere from assigning an employee a coveted work task or allowing employees greater autonomy and decision-making to a simple thank you.

The key to the effectiveness and power of informal business culture rewards and recognition is applying these three principles:

- equity, consistency, and fairness

---

3   Prosci Inc., "The Top Five Reasons Employees Resist Change." From website: www.change-management.com/tutorial-resistance-mod2.htm.

- rewarding meaningful accomplishments

- valued by employees receiving them

Front-line managers who have figured out that all three of these points must apply are usually successful both in effectively reinforcing the work behaviours and performance that they desire and in creating a loyal and motivated workforce.

The challenge is that middle and front-line management are often the most set in their ways. And they often feel the most threatened by a major organizational transformation. One reason for resistance from this level of the organization is that many have participated in other major transformations that resulted in greater autonomy to front-line staff and eroded the need for their oversight. Also, they were once the experts, the most experienced in older systems and processes. Now, skills proficiency and knowledge are creating a more level playing field, and many in middle management feel they will not have the same respect from their staff.

CREATE A SEPARATE INCENTIVE PROGRAM FOR FRONT-LINE MANAGERS

To support transformation, senior managers understand that positive reinforcement and effective rewards are important for staff but, for some reason, often do not see it as important for their front-line managers. But change at that level of the organization will not occur on its own and must be managed. Senior management needs to provide incentives for their front-line management. Much like what front-line management has done, senior management must find out what their front-line management values and reward them for reinforcing their staff performance related to the change.

Hold Front-Line Management Recognition Days

It is recommended to hold front-line management recognition days at least annually. Besides continually recognizing meaningful achievement among this group, it is an opportunity to address other business culture issues and important business.

To inaugurate the program, consider holding a separate front-line management event after the launch and just before announcing changes to formal business culture rewards and reinforcements. Advertise the day as a critical Management Review and Strategy session on managing the new transformation in the coming months. The Project Sponsor or other Senior Executive Leader should lead the event. If budget allows, hold the event at an off-site location or somewhere that sends a message that the meeting is important and participants are valued. The agenda for the day could go as follows.

TYPICAL AGENDA

1. Senior executive session kick-off

   a. Welcome and thank all front-line managers for making the difficult journey successful so far. State that you understand that front-line managers hold the key to creating a good business culture, recognizing the important job they do on the front lines.

   b. Outline the main objective of the session: to gain insight and solicit help from front-line managers for strategies to make the transformation a normal part of work culture.

   c. Present awards of recognition. State: "But first, before introducing our facilitator for the day, the Executive Team wants to formally recognize some notable achievements." The Executive Team should prepare a number of recognition awards to deserving front-line managers/supervisors for two kinds of achievements:

- significant contribution in helping create or establish the old legacy solution

- significant contribution in the development or implementation of the transformation solution

d. Introduce the assigned facilitator, to take the group through the day's agenda. This may be an occasion when you use an outside facilitator or find an internal facilitator who will be seen as neutral or impartial (a good candidate might be someone in an internal organizational development or HR role).

2. Identify the current business culture. Define business culture as "the system of shared beliefs and values that develops within an organization and guides the behaviour of its members."[4]

- Explain/give examples (stories from founding members of the organization, accepted work habits and rituals that are unique to the organization, and unique rules and roles).

- Have front-line managers characterize what makes their culture unique.

- Identify whether these cultural traits are unique to a work group/area or shared throughout the organization. (Are they part of the main organizational/

---

4   E. Schein, "Organizational Culture," *American Psychologist* 45 (1990): 109-19.

business culture or a sub-culture within a specific group?)

3. Share how business culture is reinforced and rewarded on the job. Ask front-line managers to share how they reinforce and reward these examples of shared business culture within their own work group.

4. Brainstorm ways to establish new culture of change.

    *   Discuss and list new characteristics, work behaviour, habits, etc., that must be established to make the transformation solution part of the new business culture.

    *   Identify which of the current cultural characteristics support, contradict, or are neutral to the new way of doing things being established by the recently implemented transformation solution.

    *   Discuss how front-line managers can help reinforce new characteristics back on the job.

5. Senior executive closing

    a. Thank all front-line managers for their participation.

    b. Emphasize and reiterate that front-line managers will be the ones who will have the biggest impact on making the transformation part of the new business culture.

    c. State that the suggestions given today "will be collected and shared back with the Executive Team for all to draw upon to help entrench the new business culture moving forward. Each of your senior managers will follow up with you to discuss how you will work together to make that happen."

Continue Monitoring and Measuring Transformation Solution Results

Measurements established during this step will continue to be collected and then incorporated into the strategic measurements continually reviewed by the Executive Team. The Project Sponsor must ensure that all measures established by the project are continued and included into the regular business review process. For the first six months after launch, these measures should be collected and reviewed monthly, which may be more frequent than senior management review. A senior sub-committee may need to be tasked with reviewing figures to ensure successful progress.

CONCLUSION

*The best of all leaders is the one who helps people
    so that, eventually, they don't need him.
Then comes the one they love and admire.
Then comes the one they fear.
The worst is the one who lets people push him
    around.
Where there is no trust, people will act in bad
    faith.
The best leader doesn't say much, but what he
    says carries weight.
When he is finished with his work, the people
    say, "It happened naturally."*

—Lao Tzu

T HE ABOVE QUOTE WAS intended for political or military leaders. However, the philosophy captures the essence for what should be a constant theme in the minds of all who accept leadership responsibility for major organizational transformations. Senior Leaders or Project Managers who choose not to abdicate this role to consultants must become extraordinary leaders.

Beyond understanding and applying the 10 Steps in this book, you must understand two overriding challenges that come with leading an organization through a major transformation.

Challenge #1: People Don't Like Change

A lot of research backs up this claim.[1] Unless an individual has a strong personal reason for seeking change, such as to improve an unsatisfactory situation, the majority of individuals in your organization are comfortable and confident in the tasks they do and working in their current business culture. The initial reaction to change from most will be resistance or at least skepticism. As soon as you are assigned the leadership role in a major organizational transformation, you immediately and automatically have acquired the challenge of upsetting that comfort and confidence.

Challenge #2: You Can't Motivate Anyone to Do Anything

I taught an organizational behaviour course at a local university for many years. One of the key topics of study was motivation. In every first-class discussion on motivation, I posed this question to students: "Can you motivate another individual to do something?" Most answered "yes," thinking that we must be studying motivation in an organizational behaviour class to learn about tactics to motivate employees to do things

---

1   One of the leading writers on organizational change, Rosabeth Moss Kanter, describes ten reasons why people resist change, including loss of control, loss of faith, and more work. See *Harvard Business Review* article at http://blogs.hbr.org/kanter/2012/09/ten-reasons-people-resist-chang.html.

the organization wants them to do. However, the reality is that, although organizations may get people to comply with their wishes by a number of tactics, true *motivation* comes from within. The *Oxford Dictionaries* defines motivation as "a reason or reasons for acting or behaving in a particular way."[2] However, this definition doesn't capture the essence of where those "reasons" really come from. In fact, they come from within each individual. An organization may convince individuals to perform the work activities and exhibit the behaviour required, but those actions or behaviours do not mean that the individuals are motivated. Individuals will decide what they actually believe in and what gets them excited to do something. Therefore, individuals can motivate themselves, but *you* can't motivate someone to do anything.

So what is the point of managing change? Can we really make a difference as change leaders and get people to believe in something they would not have believed in if we hadn't intervened? Or can we even get them to believe in something faster if we use the right tactics? Are we tricking them into believing something they normally would not?

Many years ago, I attended a lecture by a very famous organizational behaviour guru who addressed a small group of change management professionals. His name isn't important—but something he said is because it upset me considerably.

---

2   http://oxforddictionaries.com/definition/english/motivation

I reacted rather violently, and the experience stayed with me a long time.

He stated that change management professionals were doing a disservice to organizations, and often actually caused harm to organizations and their employees. By applying aggressive tactics to force people to change quickly, they were creating a unique form of depression among many employees called "anaclitic depression."[3] This is a form of depression that occurs when a key individual or idea that is an important support for the (affected) individual is taken away; as a result, people can emotionally waste away. He then gave a few extreme examples of horrific historical situations where individuals and regimes caused anaclitic depression. Extrapolating from those, he said that employees will go along with ideas they don't believe in to avoid the feeling of anaclitic depression and that imposing change will sometimes cause this depression to occur (when we take away their original ideal situation). Furthermore, he stated, by working to create support and commitment to the new business culture, change management professionals and change leaders often contribute to creating anaclitic depression among employees. I was simultaneously astounded and outraged that this management guru was comparing the effect of the work we do—the work I do—to what despotic leaders did to people during their reigns of terror!

Long after the lecture was delivered, I continued to think about it and my reaction, and I have come to the following conclusion: ignoring the inappropriate comparative examples the guru gave, he was trying to point out that change management professionals help change leaders develop

3   www.wisegeek.com/what-is-anaclitic-depression.htm#did-you-know

coercive tactics to make people afraid to disagree with the new status quo ... which could create this phenomenon of anaclitic depression. I believe that this may be how some change management professionals and change leaders act, but it is the wrong approach.

An effective transformation effort must be based on full and honest disclosure, and although you are selling a new way of doing things, it must be done with the realization that everyone will come to their own conclusions. It must not involve coercion or fairy-tale descriptions of how things will be in the future. Transformation leaders must spend a lot of time understanding other people's beliefs in order to make genuine connections in how the change aligns with these core beliefs and values. Sometimes, it may even involve modifying the solution to incorporate core cultural beliefs that a critical mass of people believes in.

Yes, in the end, some will really not like the solution nor want to change, but as a leader of a major change, you can address these individuals with an honest response: "We respect your opinion and beliefs [versus "you are being resistant and must comply"], but you know and understand why we must change. What can we do to make the transition as easy for you as possible? Hopefully, in time, the solution will make sense, and you will come to embrace it."

I truly believe that if you respect every employee's personal beliefs regarding the change (whether you like them or not); if you listen more than you speak so that you understand their issues, concerns, and fears; and if you incorporate everything you hear into your new business culture, then you will be on the road to achieving Lao Tzu's ultimate leadership accomplishment in your transformation:

When he is finished with his work, the people say, "It happened naturally."

Good luck in using the 10 Steps to successfully achieve your major organizational transformation and create a positive Big Change.

GLOSSARY

Adoption Rate   The number of members of a society who start using a new technology or innovation during a specific period of time. The rate of adoption is a relative measure, meaning that the rate of one group is compared with the rate of another, often of the entire society.[1]

Change Agent   A person who possesses enough knowledge, power, and/or influence to guide and facilitate the change effort.

Change Champion   A senior manager assigned as a member of a Change Champion Committee or Change Network. This individual is typically one management level below the Steering Committee members, is relied upon to help the Project Team drive the change, and ideally has the following traits:

- knows the end-to-end business operations of that function very well

- is known and respected by other employees in that function

- is a good communicator

---

1   www.investopedia.com/terms/r/rate-of-adoption.asp

- is assertive

- has a positive view of the transformation solution

Change Champion Committee A core group of senior change agents who meet as a group and work individually to share information, provide input, disseminate information, and help implement change-related activities throughout and within an organization to assist in a large organizational transformation (sometimes called a change network).

Change Management A commonly accepted definition is the application of a structured process and tools to enable individuals or groups to transition from a current state to a future state, such that a desired outcome is achieved.[2] Another definition is that large-scale organizational change is about readying the organization in changes affecting process, technology, and people. Change management focuses on getting people ready and committed in time for planned changes.

Communication Lead The Project Leader who is accountable for developing and delivering the project communication plan and activities.

Community of Practice (CoP) A group of people who share a concern or a passion for something they do and learn how to do it better as they interact regularly.

---

2   Prosci Inc. definition from website: www.prosci.com/main/change_definition.html.

Critical Mass of Support   The number of stakeholders required to create enough support for the change to create momentum and take hold in the organization. (See also **tipping point**)

Critical Path   The sequence of scheduled activities that determines the duration of the project. It is the longest path through the project.[3]

Crossover Manager   The senior manager or executive who manages all other leaders and functions affected by the proposed transformation.

Enterprise Resource Planning (ERP) Systems   Business management software that allows an organization to use a system of integrated applications to manage the business.[4]

External Stakeholder   An individual, group, or organization that is somehow impacted by or could impact the transformative change of another organization (e.g., a customer, supplier, or government agency).

Forming   The first of the four stages of team development, characterized by Team members still unsure of their roles, how to interact with the Team, and how to get things done co-operatively.

---

3   *A Guide to the Project Management Body of Knowledge* (PMBOK Guide), 4th ed.

4   www.webopedia.com/TERM/E/ERP.html

Frequently Asked Questions (FAQs)   Categorized answers to questions that typically get asked over and over by stakeholders. Often published for distribution and/or easy access.

Functional Lead   A Team Leader within a transformation project accountable for implementing one of the major processes being delivered as part of the overall transformation. For example, in a major enterprise technology implementation introducing new IT financial technology, there may be Functional Leads for the Accounts Payable and General Accounting processes.

Gates (or Gating)   The conclusion of a project phase is generally marked by (1) completion and review of both key deliverables and project performance to date, (2) determination if the project should continue into its next phase, and (3) cost-effective detection and correction of errors. These phase-end reviews are often called phase exits, stage gates, or kill points.[5]

Go-live Date   The date that the process, technology, and/or people changes become active in an organization's day-to-day business operations. For technology, it is when the 'switch' is turned on and the new system or application is in production. For processes, people are expected to now conduct work in the modified or re-engineered steps of all new processes. For people, all changes to organizational structure, job positions, or other changes to people's roles formally take effect.

---

5   PMBOK Guide, 4th ed.

High-performing Team   Teams that reach the fourth and highest level of team development (performing).

Human Resource Information System (HRIS)   A system that seeks to merge the activities associated with human resource management (HRM) and information technology (IT) into one common database through the use of Enterprise Resource Planning (ERP) software. The goal of HRIS is to merge the different parts of human resources, including payroll, labour productivity, and benefit management, into a less capital-intensive system than the mainframes used to manage activities in the past. Also called Human Resource Management Systems (HRMS).[6]

Internal Stakeholders   For a transformation project, any employee who is impacted by, or who could impact, the changes being implemented in the transformation.

Norming   The third of four stages of team development, characterized by Team members learning to interact more effectively, communicating more effectively, and dealing with issues on their own.

Performing   The fourth of four stages of team development, characterized by Team members focusing on perfecting the delivery of coordinated Team tasks. Team members are beyond having to spend time discussing issues or working out what needs to be done. In this phase, Teams know what needs to be

---

6   Businessdictionary.com: www.businessdictionary.com/definition/Human-Resource-Information-Systems-HRIS.html.

done, how to coordinate tasks between one another, and have practised many, many times to make the coordinated effort perfect.

Priority Business Culture Driver   An organizational measurement that drives work behaviour (priority decisions and work activity).

Product Owner   An individual on a technical Project Team who has overall accountability for managing the effectiveness and performance of a specific IT system or application.

Project Advocate   An executive ally who has either a strategic reason and/or a personal belief for actively supporting the project and transformation.

Project Charter   The document issued by the project initiator or Project Sponsor that formally authorizes the existence of a project and provides the Project Manager with the authority to apply organizational resources to project activities.[7] It typically includes the project context, background, full initial scope, schedule, and all other major elements of the project required to launch the project and create the initial Project Plan.

Project Coordinator   Coordinates activities and functions of a designated project to ensure that goals and objectives specified for the project are accomplished.[8]

---

7   www.ehow.com/facts_6179715_define-project-charter-purpose.html

8   www.asu.edu/aad/manuals/policyarchives/CPM/July2003/cpm002.html

Project Manager   Project Leader who has the responsibility for the planning, execution, and closing of any project. Typically reports to a Project Sponsor.

Project Plan   A plan indicating deliverables, activities, dependencies, and resources for a project.

Project Sponsor   The senior manager or executive lead of the transformation project. Key accountabilities are:

- facilitating consensus among all executive stakeholders throughout the life of the project
- communicating the new priorities to the organization
- providing the reinforcement required to ensure success
- ensuring resources requirements are met and maintained throughout the life of the project

Project Team   The group of individuals (employees and/or externally hired consultants and contractors) assigned as dedicated resources for the planning, implementation, and early launch support of a project. The Project Team will disband after all project deliverables are complete.

Project Team Lead   Any Project Team member who is accountable for leading a group of individuals in planning and implementing one or more streams of work in the project.

Project Team Member   Any dedicated member of a Project Team accountable for the planning, delivery, and/or support of the Project Team.

SAP (Systems Applications and Products in Data Processing) SAP, started in 1972 in Mannheim, Germany, by five former IBM employees, states that it is the world's largest inter-enterprise software company and the world's fourth-largest independent software supplier, overall. The original name for SAP was German—*Systeme, Anwendungen, Produkte*—meaning Systems, Applications, Products. The original SAP idea was to provide customers with the ability to interact with a common corporate database for a comprehensive range of applications. Gradually, the applications have been assembled, and today many corporations, including IBM and Microsoft, are using SAP products to run their own businesses.[9]

Stakeholder Any individual who is impacted by, or who could impact, the changes imposed by the transformation.

Stakeholder Map A comprehensive listing of all employees who will be impacted by the change, usually in both organizational structure and chart form.

Stakeholder Readiness Analysis Analysis conducted to understand what impact the transformation solution will have on each group of stakeholders and their business culture and to identify the level of support and resistance that exists for the project.

Storming The second of four stages of team development, characterized by Team members challenging both other Team members and the leadership. Arguments may ensue

---

9   http://searchsap.techtarget.com/definition/SAP

and productivity may drop, with Team members working at cross-purposes as they try to establish themselves and their norms in the Team.

Super Users   Employees selected to become experts in their work area for a new system or application being introduced. In a major technology transformation, Super Users are typically trained well in advance of the new system being introduced and launched to other users in the organization.

Technical Lead   A Project Team member who is accountable for the planning, implementation, and support of technical aspects of one or more technical streams of the transformation project (e.g., hardware, software development, interface development). This may or may not include the supervision of other resources.

Technical Testing Lead   A Project Team member who is accountable for all aspects of testing the new technology and/or processes of the transformation. In a technology transformation, this would include:

- Component Testing

- Configuration Testing

- Application Testing

- Conversion Testing

- Integration Testing

Tipping Point   The moment of critical mass, the threshold, and the boiling point. It is the point when everyday things reach epidemic proportions. There are three distinct characteristics of epidemics: contagiousness (the Law of the Few), the fact that little causes can have big effects (the Sticking Factor), and that change happens not gradually but at one dramatic moment (the Power of Context).

Training Lead   A Project Team member who is accountable for the planning, design, delivery, and support of customized training for the transformation. This individual typically will manage a team of training designers, coordinators, and deliverers.

Transformation Projects   Those projects that significantly change business processes, people processes, and/or major technological capabilities. They are typically projects that will make or break organizations. Some examples are:

- a merger or acquisition

- major organizational restructuring due to required strategic changes.

- major organizational restructuring as a result of downsizing or expansion

- a major enterprise technology change required to better operate or compete (e.g., ERP implementation)

User Acceptance Test (UAT)   The last phase of the software testing process. During UAT, actual software users test the software to make sure it can handle required tasks in real-world scenarios, according to specifications. It is one of the final and most critical software project procedures that must occur before newly developed software is rolled out to the market. UAT is also known as beta testing, application testing, or end user testing.[10] UAT is always the final testing phase of a technology transformation.

WIIFM (What's In It For Me) An acronym commonly used among change management professionals that refers to the importance of determining what benefits stakeholders believe will be realized by adapting to the changes imposed by the transformation.

---

10 www.techopedia.com/definition/3887/user-acceptance-testing-uat

ACKNOWLEDGEMENTS

I WOULD LIKE TO express my thanks to the Barlow Publishing team who, in so many ways, helped to make this book possible: to Doug Goold, who was relentless in helping me to find my "voice" in my writing; to Eleanor Gasparik, whose attention to detail made my messages clearer and more powerful; to Tracy Bordian, who helped me to stay on track and held everything together; and to Sarah Scott, whose sage advice and creative ideas helped me to make better decisions and who encouraged me throughout the publishing process.

I would also like to thank all the great leaders and talented colleagues I have referred to throughout this book—they are the ones who showed me how to manage Big Change throughout my career.

Finally, I would like to thank my family for their encouragement throughout the writing, editing, and publication of this book. I especially want to thank my wife, Lisa, who spent many hours proofreading, supporting me throughout this process, and who is my biggest inspiration.

STEVE PINKUS has played both project management and change management lead roles for major organizations in the public and private sector for close to twenty years. For ten years before that, Steve worked as the internal Project Lead for major transformation projects for organizations such as Unilever, BASF, and Caterpillar. Steve has often had a leadership role on large teams in charge of implementing major transformation projects, where the project's success often determined the organization's solvency or future growth. There are a lot of organizations and experts who claim that the roles of Project Manager and Change Management Lead in a project are two separate roles. It is Steve's contention that the Project Manager entrusted to manage and lead a major transformation should also be the Change Management Lead for that project. Project Managers and other organizational change leaders, as part of their core skill set as leaders, must understand what needs to be done to drive the change required in these transformation projects.